Old Wounds, New Words: Poems from the Appalachian Poetry Project

Old Wounds, New Words: Poems from the Appalachian Poetry Project

Edited By
Bob Henry Baber
George Ella Lyon
Gurney Norman

Introduction By
George Ella Lyon

Preface By
Jim Wayne Miller

THE JESSE STUART FOUNDATION
Ashland, Kentucky
1994

Jesse Stuart Foundation

OLD WOUNDS, NEW WORDS:
POEMS FROM THE APPALACHIAN POETRY PROJECT

Copyright © 1994 by The Jesse Stuart Foundation

Library of Congress –in–Publication Data

Old wounds, new words : poems from the Appalachian poetry project /
    edited by Bob Henry Baber, George Ella Lyon, Gurney Norman ;
    introduction by George Ella Lyon ; preface by Jim Wayne Miller.
        p.   cm.
    Summary: A collection of poems, written in the 1970s and 1980s,
    from the works of ninety poets from six states in the southern
    Appalachian region.
        ISBN 0-945084-44-7 : $9.95
        1. Young adult poetry, American—Appalachian Region, Southern.
    2. Appalachian Region, Southern—Poetry.   3. American poetry—20th
    century.   [1. Appalachian Region—Poetry.   2.   American poetry
    –Collections.]   I. Baber, Bob Henry.   II. Lyon, George Ella, 1949-
        III. Norman, Gurney,   1937-
    PS554.043   1994
    811'.540809769—dc20   94-7994
                                                                        CIP
                                                                        AC

First Edition

Published by:
The Jesse Stuart Foundation
P.O. Box 391
Ashland, KY 41114
1994

For my father, Troy Nash Baber,
and my mother, Roberta Finnegan
— Bob Henry Baber

To the poets
&
to Steve, who
supported this project
for fourteen years
with love and childcare
— George Ella Lyon

I dedicate this book
to the 20 million people
of the Appalachian Region
of North America
— Gurney Norman

The editors wish to thank:

- the Wytter-Bynner Foundation, for the grant which
  made the Appalachian Poetry Project possible
- John Stephenson and the University of Kentucky's
  Appalachian Center, for sponsoring this work during
  and beyond the grant period
- Cene Nash and Davenna Sexton, for secretarial assistance
- Delilah Conley, for proofreading
- Anne Campbell, for help in the University of Kentucky's
  Appalachian Collection
- our families for their support
- the poets for their work and their patience
- the editors and staff of small magazines and presses in the
  region, who brought much of this work to light
- the workshop leaders for gathering poets and materials

Gail Amburgey	Jeff Kiser
Maggie Anderson	P. J. Laskin
Joy Bannerman	Fred Milner
Mary Joan Coleman	Mary Jane Putzel
Sydney Farr	Barbara Smith
Madeline Flannery	Bob Snyder
Marita Garin	Renee Stamper
Peggy Hall	John Coward
Pauletta Hansel	Jim Webb
Lee Howard	Jack Wright

PREFACE

It is rare for a collection of poems to await publication for more than a decade. Rare, but not unprecedented. In 1986 the Jesse Stuart Foundation published Stuart's *Songs of a Mountain Plowman*, poems written between 1929 and 1931, which, I discovered in the process of editing them, are a kind of rehearsal and preparation for Stuart's *Man With a Bull-Tongue Plow* (1934), long thought to be Stuart's first book of poems. *Songs of a Mountain Plowman*, which shed new light on Stuart's development as a poet, awaited publication for over half a century.

With the hope that, like Stuart's early work, it will contribute to a deeper understanding and wider appreciation of the history and culture of Stuart's native southern Appalachia, the Jesse Stuart Foundation now makes available *Old Wounds, New Words: Poems from the Appalachian Poetry Project*, a collection of poems that has gone unpublished since 1981.

The story of how *Old Wounds, New Words* began, grew, and then languished unpublished for years is already a part of southern Appalachia's literary history, and has been re-counted and documented by Chris Green, a student at the Gaines Center for the Humanities at the University of Kentucky.[1] The collection was initiated in 1979 by a grant from the Witter Bynner Foundation, Santa Fe, New Mexico, to promote poetry in the Appalachian region.

Gurney Norman, recently returned from California to assume the position of writer-in-residence at the University of Kentucky, became Director of the Appalachian Poetry Project, which was administered from the University of Kentucky's Appalachian Center. Norman was joined by George Ella Lyon, who became the project's Executive Director, and Bob Henry Baber, Field Organizer and Coordinator. In 1980, using as their initial contacts members of the Southern Appalachian Writers Cooperative (SAWC), Norman, Lyon and Baber held 19 exciting and highly successful poetry workshops in the Appalachian areas of six states. Lyon and Baber then read through the poems generated by the workshops with a view to preparing a manuscript for publication. (Later they also gleaned work by other Appalachian poets from magazines and journals dating back to 1970.) The result was an anthology of work by 91 poets from the southern Appalachian region with a graceful and insightful introduction by Lyon.

Although the collection was, as Baber described it, "probably one of the most inclusive grassroots anthologies that ever was compiled in the U.S.," its editors experienced frustration and disappointment in their efforts to find a publisher. Regional presses were not interested in publishing poetry. State arts councils were reluctant to support publication because the anthology included writers from other states.

Then, at one point in the 1980s, fortune seemed to smile on the project. The editors were so certain that *Old Wounds, New Words* would be published by the Institute for the Study of Southern Culture at the University of Mississippi that publication parties were held and announcements were sent to the poets who had contributed to the anthology. But two years later the book was still unpublished and the Institute's commitment had evaporated.

Time passed. Another publisher was found in Charleston, West Virginia. A second publication party was held. The editors circulated the news release announcing *Old Wounds, New Words* imminent appearance. Because of the Charleston publisher's decision to publish the collection in a spiral binder instead of a perfect binding, as originally planned, the editors withdrew the collection.

And there the matter stood. Although the manuscript had circulated as a kind of Appalachian *samizdat* or underground writing in poetry workshops, and although its introduction had been used in Appalachian literature courses, *Old Wounds, New Words*, something of a mystery anthology, remained unpublished more than a decade after the search for a publisher had begun.

It is understandable that in their frustration and disappointment the editors referred to the anthology as "the child that never got born," "a baby we've lost." Actually, they never gave up trying to find a publisher more appropriate than any they previously applied to.

Now *Old Wounds, New Words* comes to us like a 1980-model automobile in mint condition! It represents the poetry landscape that existed in Appalachia ten, fifteen, and even twenty years ago. The work of some poets might not seem representative of them now. But it seemed so at one time and so it stands here—along with notes that have not been updated past the mid-1980s. Some of the contributors—Jo Carson, Kathyrn Stripling Byer, Fred Chappell, Robert Morgan—have developed remarkably over the years and received much deserved recognition for distinguished work. Like the writers who preceeded them in Appalachia—Byron Herbert Reece, James Still, Elizabeth Madox Roberts, Jesse Stuart—many of the poets of *Old Wounds, New Words* have written successfully in other genres—the short story, novel, drama. Some have moved to other parts of the country—Lee Howard, Betsy Sholl. Some are deceased—Joe Barrett, Lillie D. Chaffin, Louise McNeill.

To some extent *Old Wounds, New Words* resembles a time

capsule whose contents suggest the way things were at some point in the past. But the collection isn't, finally, the baby that never was born, or the automobile from the 1980s in mint condition, or the time capsule with a newspaper headline from a past decade. Good poetry, like other kinds of literature, is not news, or, if so, it is news that stays news. Good writing, no matter how old, seems fresh and new, as is suggested by a letter to the New York publisher of Homer's *Odyssey* in paperback. The letter writer, a young man in South Dakota, assumed The *Odyssey's* author was contemporary. "Let's have more stories by this guy Homer. He can write!"

We are told that the light seen when we look up at stars in the night sky started coming to us long ago, and that in some cases, the light just now arriving is from stars that have gone out. Doesn't this notion suggest the better metaphor for *Old Wounds, New Words*? Although these poems, like light from stars, started coming to us years ago, they arrive just now. Look at them.

Jim Wayne Miller

[1] Chris Green, "Coscientizacao: A Theory of Community in Little Magazines." Thesis for the Gaines Center for the Humanities.m Lexington, KY: University of Kentucky. April, 1991.

CONTENTS

Old Wounds, New Words:

Source and Directions

George Ella Lyon

At the beginning of 1960, you could have counted the important Appalachian poets on both hands. Since then, over seventy collections of Appalachian poetry have appeared; anthologies and little magazines have featured it, and scholars have written essays about it. This sudden flowering is impressive, and, because some of the earlier poets are out of print, may seem miraculous. But it has its roots in work that came before, in individual voices, and in what they expressed for the region as a whole.

I

Ballad of the Bones, Hounds on the Mountain, Song in the Meadow—the titles of these books of Appalachian poetry from the thirties and forties reveal its origin in closeness to the earth and love of song. These collections by Byron Herbert Reece of north Georgia, and James Still and Elizabeth Madox Roberts of Kentucky, are rooted in tradition, formally as well as thematically. They contain sonnets, ballads, song cycles, and carefully reined free verse, often with a biblical cadence. While they employ less dialect than Ann Cobb's groundbreaking *Kinfolks: Kentucky Mountain Rhymes* (1922), they show a kinship to those poems, to Roy Helton's *Lonesome Waters* (1930), and to Jesse Stuart's *Man with a Bull-Tongue Plow* (1934), in that they wish to examine and most often to preserve the stories and values that have been islanded within the culture as a whole. As James Still writes in "White Highways":

1

I have gone out to the roads that go up and down
In smooth white lines, stoneless and hard;
I have seen distances shortened between two points,
The hills pushed back and bridges thrust across
The shallow river's span.

To the broad highways, and back again I have come
To the creek-bed roads and narrow winding trails
Worn into ruts by hoofs and steady feet;
I have come back to the long way around,
The far between, the slow arrival.
Here is my pleasure most where I have lived
And called my home.
                    O do not wander far
From the rooftree and the hill-gathered earth;
Go not upon these wayfares measured with a line
Drawn hard and white from birth to death.
O quiet and slow is peace, and curved with space
Brought back again to this warm homing place.[1]

Still's "homing place" is quiet in the world's sense, away
from frantic machines and rapid transit, but it is lapped in
music: "The dulcimer sings from fretted maple throat" ("Moun-
tain Dulcimer"), we hear "the mellow banjos of the hounds'
throats," and "shrill notes of a sheep's horn billow down the
mountain" ("Fox Hunt"). Most importantly, the human songs
are handed down and sung, and the song comes to symbolize
identity, not just personal but cultural, the unbroken strand
of life. Byron Herbert Reece not only writes of those singing
the ballads, but also casts many of his poems in the ballad
mold, emphasizing the timelessness of his themes, the beauty
of song, and its power of renewal:

Mountain Fiddler

I took my fiddle
That sings and cries
To a hill in the middle
Of Paradise.

I sat at the base
Of a golden stone
In that holy place
To play alone.

I tuned the strings
And began to play,
And a crowd of wings
Were bent my way.
A voice said
Amid the stir:
"We that were dead,
O Fiddler,

"With purest gold
Are robed and shod,
And we behold
The face of God.

"Our halls can show
No thing so rude
As your horsehair bow,
Or your fiddlewood;
"And yet can they
So well entrance
If you but play
Then we must dance!"[2]

Song is a loom for weaving together the joys and sorrows of the earth, for shaping the human story. And narrative threads its way through the lyrical work of these poets, as though the ballad has not yet split into written forms of lyric and narrative. Notice how the light dance of rhythms in "When Daniel Was a Blacksmith," by Elizabeth Madox Roberts, prepares us for a new look at the story of Daniel Boone and plays against the heaviness of our standard image of him. In form and fable quality the poem is reminiscent of Blake:

When Daniel Was a Blacksmith

When Daniel was a blacksmith
He fitted for the dray horse,
He shod the little wild colt,
And shod the dappled gray.

When all the nags were fitted well,—
Blow, flame, thump and tap,—
He bent the iron on the forge
And pounded out a trap.

When D. Boone was a blacksmith
He walked before the rising suns.
He blew the flame and bent the steel
And mended rifle guns.

And the wild beasts in a thousand hills,
And in a thousand valley-prongs,
They lifted up their quivering ears
To hear his anvil songs.[3]

Roberts, best known for her fiction (*The Great Meadow*, 1930), is a central Kentucky native whose work often deals with Appalachian themes and experiences. In "Love in the Harvest" she writes of "a song in the meadow and a song in the mouth."[4] Certainly her fellow poets—Still, Reece, Cobb, Helton, and Stuart—find in nature's song, the "song in the meadow," the impulse for human expression, the "song in the mouth." Jesse Stuart makes this relationship explicit in his introductory poem to *Man with a Bull-Tongue Plow* (1934), a collection which further illustrates the strain of romanticism in Appalachian poetry. If his proclamation seems defensive or willfully provincial, consider that he was launching his poems on the same stream as Hart Crane and T.S. Eliot. A literary world which had seen *The Bridge* (1930) and *Ash Wednesday* (1930) was not likely to praise the "farmer singing at the plow":

Sir:

I am a farmer singing at the plow
And as I take my time to plow along
A steep Kentucky hill, I sing my song—
A one-horse farmer singing at the plow!
I do not sing the songs you love to hear;
My basket songs are woven from the words
Of corn and crickets, trees and men and birds.
I sing the strains I know and love to sing.

And I can sing my lays like singing corn,
And flute them like a fluting gray corn-bird,
And I can pipe them like a hunter's horn—
All of my life these are the songs I've heard.
And these crude strains no critic can call art,
Your very respectively, Jesse Stuart.[5]

Louise McNeill's *Gauley Mountain* (1939) marks a change in this pattern of poets singing the land, for its impulse is more narrative than lyrical, and the story of the land emerges through the stories of the people. The relationship between the two is still crucial, but the emphasis has changed. With the focus on story comes a new concern with character, not just of heroes or ballad figures, but of everyday people. The poem with which *Gauley Mountain* closes brings the human stories, with all their urgency, to rest in the hill's shadow, but there is evidence already of the difference human values are making in the landscape:

The River

. . . .

Along the shore where passing Mingo warriors
Built drift-wood fires to parch Ohio maize
Coke ovens glare red-eyed upon the darkness
And belch their cinders at the fevered days.

. . . .

. . .White herons sleep, their folded wings unstained
By all that blood the savage Gauley drained
From pale-faced men whose kindred now possess
The last dark current of the wilderness.[6]

The uneasiness evidenced in this poem increases as we come closer to our own time, and the relationship between nature and song in Appalachian poetry changes more profoundly. It is not just that the poets are disconnected from the land—though some are, and clearly that is the movement of the culture—it is that the land no longer presents itself as a constant, the hub of the wheel of seasons, of present and past, of birth and death, struggle and fulfillment. Improper road-building, damming and timbering, as well as the onslaught of strip mining, have changed the land and the lives

6

lived on it dramatically. Lifting up one's eyes unto the hills becomes less comforting when the hills stand in need of help. Folksinger Jean Ritchie chronicles the change in "Black Waters":

> O the quail, she's a pretty bird, she sings a sweet tongue;
> In the roots of the tall timbers she nests with her young.
> But the hillside explodes with the dynamite's roar,
> And the voices of the small birds will sound there no
> more;
> And the hillsides come a-sliding so awful and grand,
> And the flooding black waters rise over my land.
>
> Sad scenes of destruction on every hand;
> Black waters, black waters run down through the land.[7]

Alongside the exploitation of the land has come an accelerated modernization of life in the mountains. The speed and scale of this change, along with the economic roller-coaster of coal production and increasing industrialization, make for a very unstable way of life. As Mike Clark explains in his foreword to *Voices from the Mountains*, "The real story of Appalachia today is the attempt by mountain people to retain the humanistic elements of the old culture and at the same time to adapt to the pressures and demands of a technological society."[8]

As in James Still's "White Highways," the road is often seen as both a symbol and an agent in this transformation. Billy Edd Wheeler, West Virginia poet, playwright, and songwriter, whose *Song of a Woods Colt* appeared in 1969, gives one version of this in "The Coming of the Roads":

> O look how they've cut all to pieces
> Our ancient poplar and oak

And the hillsides are stained with the greases
That burn up the heavens with smoke

We used to curse the bold crewmen
Who stripped our earth of its ore
Now you've changed and you've gone over to them
And you've learned to love what you hated before

Once I thanked God for my treasure
Now, like rust, it corrodes
And I can't help from blaming
Your going
On the coming
The coming of the roads.[9]

In *Train Horn* Kentucky poet Lee Pennington captures a more ambivalent attitude, this time toward the railroad which hauls away the life-product of the Harlan County train watchers and gives only longing in return:

. . . .

I have seen them down at the crossing,
their eyes dug out with silence,
their mouths hanging caves on faces
and their feet tapping rhythm of train horn blow.[10]

II

The movement of contemporary Appalachian poetry, then, is from a rooted, traditional body of work to a more volatile, politically active, and varied offering. Not that there was not political awareness before, most obviously in Georgia poet Don West's *Clods of Southern Earth* (1946), a collection which exposes the condition of workers in factories, on sharecropped farms, in the mines, and in the steel mills, where West himself worked. But the political considerations which inspired songwriters like Florence Reece had not been a major source of poetry in the mountains. From the mid-sixties on, not only labor movement questions but also the old interest in and involvement with the land demanded more political thinking. It became clear that Granny had to walk uphill just to throw water off the back porch, and as Jim Wayne Miller, poet, critic, and one of the central voices of the seventies, tells us in "Small Farms Disappearing in Tennessee,"* possession of a small farm turned into a countercultural act.

Given the opposing forces at work in Appalachian life—the long-lived isolation which preserved ignorance along with strong family ties, the volatile coal economy with its exploitation of human and natural resources, the accelerated modernization and the accompanying loss—it is not surprising that its poetry offers varied and often contradictory visions. While one can say that in general it is less traditional in form, less given to the use of dialect, and more diverse in voice and rhythm than the poetry which led up to it, it is difficult to characterize more specifically than that. Two things can safely be said. First, it most often concerns itself with revaluation or reclamation of the past, which includes a strengthening or at least an exploration of the bonds between generations. Second, its strong tie to the land has continued, whether in the pastoral work of poets like Jeff Daniel Marion, Robert Morgan, Fred Chappell, and Maggie Anderson, or the more consciously political poems of Jonathan Williams, P. J. Laska, Mary Joan Coleman, and Bob Snyder.

This recognition of the bond between generations (usually the speaker in the poem and someone older), while it may be celebratory, painful, angry, or a combination thereof, is a way of remapping the land, reforesting so that the past does not erode into floods of present isolated ego. We see examples of this in the work of two young West Virginia poets, Bob Henry Baber and Mary Joan Coleman,** who were part of the Soupbean Collective, a group of writers at Antioch College/Appalachia in Beckley, West Virginia[11]

Where Baber's and Coleman's poems have the active quality of film, Tennessee poet and editor Jeff Daniel Marion's work is closer to still life.*** Contemplative, generally low-toned, his poems approach the past and the joining of generations in a different way from Baber and Coleman, but the poets share many of the same concerns.

In Marion's work, the past as a source or way to a source of life is accessible at least in the rhythms of the earth, of rising water. Often the speaker is able to carry out the commands of the past because basic facts of the landscape have remained constant and he has kept his life tuned to them. A life tuned to the stripped landscapes of eastern Kentucky or West Virginia is apt to produce more jagged lines. The threat of overburden is constant, as many protest songs tell us. Mike Kline's "Strip Away," based on "Swing Low, Sweet Chariot," is particularly effective:

> Strip away, big D-9 Dozer,
> Comin' for to bury my home,
> I'm a-gettin' madder as you're gettin' closer,
> Comin' for to bury my home.[12]

The wedding in this song of an old hymn of hope with a vision of future hopelessness is significant, an effort to graft present powerlessness onto the strength of the past and thus

---

*This poem appears in *Voices from the Hills*, ed. Robert J. Higgs and Ambrose N. Manning (New York: Ungar, 1975), pp 350-51.

** See "Roofing for Aunt Pearl" and "the man of stones," pp 25 and 48 in text.

***See "Ebbing & Flowing Spring," p 98 in text.

regain power. And some power lies in declaring the truth, whether or not action is possible. This is a recurring message in the poetry of P. J. Laska, West Virginia writer, social critic, and editor of *The Unrealist*. His "Follow-up Report from Farmington" deals with the devastation resulting from deep mining, reminding us that the enemy is more subtle than dozers or the enormous power shovel called Big Bertha:

> First the high school cracked,
> one whole wing separated,
> and the kids had to be bussed
> to schools in nearby towns.
> The basements of the houses
> began to crumble
> and floors sagged;
> a few walls leaned precariously.
> The field on the hillside
> behind the cemetery opened up—
> a deep narrow hole
> with no bottom.
> Sanders' horse wandered there
> to graze
> before they fenced it off
> and fell in.
> By the time they hauled him out
> he'd suffocated.
> Bethlehem Steel wouldn't pay anything
> because those worked out sections
> under the town
> filled up with water,
> and now nobody can go down there
> to prove that they pulled out
> those pillars of coal
> they were supposed to leave standing.

> Everybody here knows they did it,
> because the men that worked
> that part of Idamay mine
> under Farmington have said so.[13]

The force of this poem is its revelation of a truth that victims know but can do nothing about. The situation is a little more hopeful in Lillie D. Chaffin's "Old-Timer to Grandchild,"**** despite its recognition that to some extent mountain people have signed on the dotted line of their own destruction.

While it is evident that people cannot "go into backup" on any large scale, at least not unless the economy collapses, they can offer a personal resistance by declaring the truth, as in "Farmington" and "Old-Timer," and by "holding onto their rights, both mineral and otherwise," as Lee Howard says in the dedication of her book *The Last Unmined Vein* (1980). The speaker in the title poem refuses to sell coal from under his farm "to make steel in Ohio / turn on the lights in New York City / and heat houses in Detroit" because he knows the consequences. He sends the buyer away, knowing:

> ...he'll be back
> but probably after I'm dead and gone
> and if the children want to be so foolish
> as to put an end
> to what came long before them
> ain't nothing I can do about it then
> but I been laying plans
> to remind them
> of what it's gonna cost them
> I done got my marker
> and laid out the lines for my grave

****See p 43 of text.

right smack in the middle
of that vein
They gonna have to chip out the coal 6 foot by 6
and then put her right back on top of me
and that will be the end of that[14]

The best the speaker (and the poet) can do is "remind
them/ of what it's gonna cost them," the speaker by his own
dead body and the poet by the body of her work.

III

That the acceleration of change in the mountains is also
an acceleration of loss is clear. Why this change and loss should
result in a burgeoning of poetry in the last decade is not so
obvious. If there are ten names that must be mentioned in
discussing Appalachian poetry up to 1960, there are at least
thirty of significance since then, most of whom published
primarily between 1969 and 1980. There are complex reasons
for this. Along with the increased political awareness char-
acteristic of the nation as a whole in the sixties came the
growing consciousness of Appalachia as a region, a realization
from within that its distinctiveness and importance were
being distorted and sold in the *Beverly Hillbillies* market and
praised and misunderstood by outreach programs, govern-
mental and religious; that the people, like the land, were being
stripped of their ore. From the outside, Appalachia attracted
mercenaries and missionaries; from the inside, Appalachians
wondered if the War on Poverty were being waged against
them, if their lives were both quaint and deplorable, like the
little shellacked outhouses sold in Mountain Kraft stores. A
cultural crisis resulted, and it is still going on.

Poetry, so often considered impractical, a luxury, is in fact
a natural human response in dealing with this loss and
distortion of value. Through intense selectivity in imagery,

in rhythm, in sound and in word, poetry calls forth value; its light shines on the few things chosen till they become luminous, radiating a truth long locked within. By the sheer act of naming, poetry declares what is lasting and eases the mortality of people and places it is concerned with. By rendering us speechful, poetry incants us, and the incantation both recognizes and bestows value.

The obvious question is, why poetry? Isn't this valuing process part of all literature which is essentially, however desperate, an act of affirmation? Certainly, but poetry is the logical vehicle here for many reasons. To begin with, its intensity matches the feeling of crisis and its immediacy—it is not, after all, as time-consuming as fiction—matches the urgency of the situation. Poetry is also a natural development of expression in a song- and story-fed culture.

More importantly, poetry is rooted in paradox, and paradox is as indigenous to Appalachia as the coal: wealth and poverty (personal, cultural, ecological), beauty and ugliness, the stereotype with its wink of truth. The violent good neighbor, loving father who puts a fork in his boy's arm at the dinner table. Steady, wise hill farmer who would like to burn up all the kids in the university before they burn it down themselves. Straight-forward corruption—revivalist who saves a new wife every night. People so poor their new baby sleeps in the box of their color TV, people starving to death behind the wheel of a car, people whose lives are up on blocks, gutted, rusted out. All these leaves and seeds of paradox fall down that steep air and rot into rich ground where poetry can take hold, for the energy of poetry lies in language and paradox. The force of metaphor comes from its wedding of like and unlike to make something new without destroying the separate identities of the old. It is easy to see how this approaches the dilemma of Appalachia itself.

Poetry offers, then, some healing, a map of relatedness amid the fragmentation and isolation of modern life and the template sameness that is its deadening connector. Furthermore, its recognition of paradox, its mission work among the irreconcilable forces in our lives, is a form of healing. And, to the extent that to name and to tell are to know and thus to control, poetry gives us a measure of power over those forces.

NOTES

[1] James Still, *Hounds on the Mountain* (New York: Viking Press, 1937), p. 45.

[2] Byron Herbert Reece, *Ballad of the Bones* (New York: E.P. Dutton, 1945), p. 56.

[3] Elizabeth Madox Roberts, *Song in the Meadow* (New York: Viking Press, 1940), p. 98.

[4] Roberts, p. 26.

[5] Jesse Stuart, *Man with a Bull-Tongue Plow* (New York: E.P. Dutton, 1934), p. 3.

[6] Louise McNeill, *Gauley Mountain* (New York: Harcourt Brace, 1939), p. 98.

[7] Jean Ritchie, "Black Waters" (New York: Geordie Music Publishing Co., 1967).

[8] Mike Clark, "Appalachia: The Changing Times," Foreword to *Voices from the Mountains*, collected and recorded by Guy and Candie Carawan (New York: Knopf, 1975), p. ix.

[9] Billy Edd Wheeler, *Song of a Woods Colt* (Anderson, S.C.: Droke House, 1969), p. 106.

[10] Lee Pennington, *Scenes from a Southern Road* (Smithtown, N.Y.: JRD Publishing Co., 1969), p. 45.

[11] Baber's book, *Assorted Life Savers*, appeared in 1976 and Coleman's *Take One Blood Red Rose* in 1978, but both poets' work had appeared earlier in the Antioch/Appalachia literary magazine *What's a Nice Hillbilly Like You....?* and in works published by the Southern Appalachian Writer's Cooperative, which they helped to found. SAWC sought to form a network of writers in the region in order to overcome the problems of isolation, the reluctance of publishers, and the obstacles to truth-telling which they all felt. In 1977, they published *Soupbean: An Anthology of Contemporary Appalachian Literature* and *New Ground*, an anthology co-published with *Mountain Review*, the Appalshop magazine out of Whitesburg,

Kentucky. In 1978, SAWC published *Mucked,* a collection of writings and photographs in response to the 1977 flooding of Appalachia.

While the Soupbean poets are no longer a group, SAWC is still holding on, most recently with the help of the Appalachian Poetry Project, a year-long effort supported by a grant to the University of Kentucky's Appalachian Center from the Witter Bynner Foundation, to encourage poetry in the mountains. The project held eighteen reading/workshops in a five-state area. Many of these were led by old Soupbean and SAWC poets whose work appears in the most recent SAWC publication, *Strokes: Contemporary Appalachian Poetry* (1980).

With support of the Appalachian Poetry Project, a meeting to regroup was held November 13-15, 1981, at the Highlander Center in New Market, Tennessee, and SAWC members, old and new, discussed the role of SAWC for the eighties.

[12] Mike Kline, "Strip Away" in *Voices from the Mountains,* P. 36.

[13] P.J. Laska, *Songs and Dances* (Prince, W. Va.: Unrealist Press, 1977), p. 30.

[14] Lee Howard, "The Last Unmined Vein" in *The Last Unmined Vein* (Washington, D.C.: Anemone Press, 1980), pp. 50-51.

Old Wounds, New Words: Poems from the Appalachian Poetry Project

SORGHUM HARVEST

As the day goes swiftly
your life goes
unlike the plodding horse
following the lead pole
slowly turning the sweep
keeping the mill rollers in motion
methodically crushing the cane.
With summer waning
you feel your life passing
unlike the slow ooze
of cane juice strained by burlap
unlike the slow barrel fill
beneath the boom pole's turning
turning while you think of planting
the seven seeds to a hill
the first sight of shoots emerging
the upward growth of stalks and leaves
the thinning of the stalks
the sun and rain and red seeds hardening
leading to this harvest
of which you are a part
watching the cane juice
boil from green to caramel.

The summer is ending
but there will be the thick pour
of sorghum on hot buttered toast.

— *Ray Allen*

BLOOD MONEY

This blood rolling down my arm
is from the wounds of a dollar bill
that cut my fingers as I touched it,
The blood runs down my elbows
and drips off onto the sand.
Mr. Pittston is kicking dirt over it,
swearing
there are no names written
on that dollar bill.

All this is the result
of thinking too much
about a Law Suit
proving me of
"The Survival Syndrome":
I get money
but none of the dead are resurrected.

— *Gail Amburgey*

3 A.M. TRAIN

the whistle blows
on the 3 a.m. train
 and stops at the graveyard

it seems as though
the railroad cars
are loading up souls
along with the coal

Souls of dead miners
that owe their essence
to that life-giving cinder

the consistency and cadence
in the wheels carry
the long
distant
hollowing
flute-like bellow
and show me the shame
that isn't mine
but my father's
and his father before him.

an uncle killed
from clearing out
that dead black coal.
and I close my eyes
and see his corpse
loaded onto his
destiny.

— *Gail Amburgey*

THE BEANS

Are climbing everywhere. I haven't staked them
and they're latching onto whatever will help them grow:
the handle of the rake I left out all night; the front
wheel of the old rusted machine by the fence line; the
tall weeds behind them; each other.

And their desperate pushing is faintly crazy. In
the way we are all crazy when we try to remember
where it was that this happened before in just this
way. Like a suicide rummaging for razor blades, a
deaf man teaching himself to whistle.

— *Maggie Anderson*

FOR THE ANNIVERSARY OF
MY FATHER'S DEATH

Today is the last time I shall speak to you.
Now I shall cease speaking to you, my relative.
-from a Fox Indian chant to the dead

It has been one year. The wood on your casket
must have started to decay. There is a stone at the
head of your grave for safe passage of your soul, and
poinsettias from my uncle, your brother, who wishes
you that.

You, dead, in your blue suit, on a mattress and
pillow, with those brown spots on your hands, around
your mouth and eyes. You are harder to see now.
Someone else lives in your house.

24

But I can still see large plates with birds on
them. They are arranged around a table, with a brown
lace tablecloth, waiting for friends to arrive. There
will be a party. And I can see sweat stains on a brown
chair, a red bathrobe, two red pencils on a formica
tabletop, three blue candles, a pile of newspapers, a
black umbrella. Still, I tell you, my father, I will
not die yet.

This new year will begin with my hands steady;
the energy begins in my feet. There is a wheel above
my left eye that has started to turn again. I will
speak. This is the first song; this is the last song.
This is the last song for you.

— *Maggie Anderson*

ROOFING FOR AUNT PEARL

"They want me t' move t' town,"
bent over her cane and squinting
up at me covered with stop-leak and tar,
holding hot rolled roof,
"but a told 'em,"
her palsied hand's finger
pointing to the soil,
"that I'm Cold Knob born,
Cold Knob bred,
'n' when I die, by God
I'm gonna be Cold Knob dead!"

— *Bob Henry Baber*

APPALACHIAN SPRING
(pay water bills here)

In this occupied territory
made war upon,
terrorists set blasts
making mole hills out of mountains—

six-weeks-till-frost
and Jack-in-the-Pulpit
supplanted by Sericea lespedeza.
*****

Stripped of recourse the rivers succumb
surrender rags hung from flood
till dogwood bloom—

for every kickback, a kick.
*****

Blood splashes on bark
mark the lines of demarcation-
the backside of glazed gob pile
no buffer of trees can mask
looming ever ready
to bequest its over burdened truth
next rain—

peaks above
falling prey to dozers
driven by kin
against their wills.

— *Bob Henry Baber*

A SECTION OF THE OCONEE NEAR WATKINSVILLE

Before I get in,
the aluminum canoe floats flat on the shine
of water. Then I ruin
its poise. Middle of the first shoal, though,
I'm out, stumbling through the ankle-breaking rocks.
Canoe, free-floating downstream without decision or paddle.
I lunge and bruise across the shallows to get a forefinger
in the rope eye on the stern.
June afternoon light, June afternoon water.
I know there's a life being led in lightness
out of my reach, and discipline.
I keep trying to climb in its words
and so unbalance us both.
The teacher's example is everywhere open
like a boat never tied up, no one in it,
that drifts day and night, metallic dragonfly
above the sunken log.

— *Coleman Barks*

BROOMSTRAW

Robert Penn Warren once borrowed a corpse-washing
from Andrew Lytle who borrowed from Jim Hitt.
In all three the men at a wake
undress a rigor-mortised male, lean him
against the wall, his feet in a big tub
of soap and water, and scrub energetically, up
and down, back and front, with a broom dipped in the
bucket.

There's a web of tiny root-hairs everywhere. Then the
broom's hundreds of packets from the ground, a whole field,
working the feel of that stiff crowd
through the handle into the hand. This is the work
that cleans the dead for singing,
and the sitting around drinking and talking
that's about to start.

— *Coleman Barks*

FAINTING ANGELS

you feign sleep though you hear the dream approach
through the peas and train depots
of your shrill summer garden-

your lover rolls over and sighs

in thermals of your nudity you are lured
onto the dizzy scaffolding of a gothic cathedral-
the sun dims behind burgundy clouds-
trash swirls in empty ball parks-

not rising nor falling, there is a radiation
of motion-

you see your father's hat blow off in a park
and roll on its brim among winter pigeons-

you see an airport of leaning hangers,
the hoop of the wind socks indicating all directions-
grass flutters through cracks in the runway-

you are breathless-
pathetic women with empty purses look at curtains
in the five and dime-
on the spot you declare yourself mad-

you sit delirious in a chili diner
fending off religious apparitions,
watching the lurid waitress toss her hair
as she opens a refrigerator of horrible loneliness-

you gaze into the sandstorm at your fingertips-
and you see your body dismembered in lip stick
brightness-
your rib cage blows from your vision
which refocuses slowly on lemon pies
melted in cellophane-

the waitress looks out the window
on the cricket cricket small town street-
she ignores you-

she tosses her hair-
you say good-night
and whistle half heartedly out the door

someone up the block
screams a jungle fragrance-

you walk toward it-

you see a man beating his wife in a wicked kitchen-
a dog barks among the fireflies

— *Joseph Barrett*

JOHN BERRYMAN'S BRIDGE

in minnesota
there is the skeleton
     of a rainbow
collapsed across the
     mississippi-
you can walk it
     from tip to tail
and O mr. bones
     you was right,
no gold at either end

— *Joseph Barrett*

12/31/59 - 1/1/70

There's no motel
on top of Giant
just two nylon tents
tautly applauding
forty some odd peaks
Lake Champlain
and four of us

Haskins says Saigon Saigon Saigon
until the echoes go slipping north
across the St. Lawrence

Haskins calls the photo of it
Yippies on Everest
but its just us
planting a bandana
instead of a flag
Behind us in the haze
you can see Marcy, Whiteface and the others
you can see Haskins
coming in drunk from the DC bars
in his old Triumph
across Memorial Bridge
into Arlington
with the top down

I got the snapshots blown up
and put them on the wall
beside the woodstove
they're all there

In mostly different shades
of stainless steel grey
like glacial ponds
above the tree line
like ricepaddies

We are coming in
from the DC bars
we are coming in
from the coastal camps
of the Carolinas
Haskins especially
is coming in from Vietnam

Tomorrow we will be coming in
from this acre of summit
this acre of quiet grey stone
on top of Giant

— *Joe Basilone*

MY FATHER'S BLACK LUNGS

"Rage, rage against the dying of the light."
Dylan Thomas

I

The Mingo blast furnaces
hell-fire reflections on the Ohio,
starless nights, lights in the air
like a luminous New York skyline—
seventy years of smoke and graphite
have eaten his lungs,
or is it the despair
and boredom of the unemployed
that flatten him in a bedroom
soaked in shadow?
I wish him good fortune
before he dies—
a lottery ticket for a million
dollars, a patented invention,
the attention of an important
someone, for love is not enough.

II

Everyday
he maps the ocean
floor, taking pebbles
from his pocket
to mark the site
of sunken ships
and treasures.

He stoops and
measures all his
wealth in dreams
which the current
sweeps away.

III

Somewhere he lost it:
the red center
which contains
the control switch.
Off, on — off, on,
all day he cries
over pains in his eyes.
Real blindness covers
imagined blindness
better than glasses
or a new lens made
for fingertips.
— He lost it:
the god-wad center
that holds the edge
against the knife
that slices dreams
in two like a guillotine
hitting a small fruit;
pear-drop soft, it
explodes in a basket.

IV

On the other end
of the line, black

worm for voices,
he speaks in a slur.
Slow words pity
his hardened lungs.
"Candles eat oxygen."
He has nothing else
to say. Sick Narcissus,
he swallows pills with water,
still fascinated only by
his own reflection.
Doctors prescribe
remedies, twenty capsules
a day for pain,
anxiety and sleep —
numbing the brain
as snow blankets
the jagged mountain.
A bed with headboard
filled with bottles
of tranquilizers —
black and green
screens against feeling,
and no one knows that
he is drowning
in the mirror.

V

Time has touched his face
like the autumn breeze
shaking the last
full trees.
The wind reaps
the seed he planted,

leaving a harvest
of barren ground.

VI

Like a child with croup
he sucks the air.
I stand there
against the wall
of the darkened hallway
and listen to each breath,
loving him, wishing that
he understood what went wrong
or even what went right
as he slips easy,
all too easy,
into that good night.

— *Carley Rees Bogarad*

AN INTERPRETATION

You peel my clothes
as though skinning an
onion-
You do this
just as you did all
those day dreams
ago-

This and thus it
goes-
Now I'm as nude
as a buttercup
Raw as a sore
As ordinary as a
thumb-

And you thought it
would be exciting-

— *Susan Burgess*

GHOST STORY

My grandmother's ghost
stalks these mountains
in high button shoes
and the silk skirt she wore
when she flirted with cowboys
and wild Irish miners
who came north to strike
it rich quick in the Black Hills
where winter was fiercer
than even the coldest ones here
in the tame Appalachians
she later called home.
On her deathbed she sighed
for the mountains of Brasstown,
Dahlonega, even the ridge
of the Balsams she'd seen
only once from a passing
car. Thirty years
she cursed the heat
of south Georgia, the flies,
and the infernal gossip
that branded her. Unsmiling
she walked the small streets.
Now she stalks these mountains
from Big Fork to Snowbird,
her shoe buttons gleaming,
her silk skirt a cloud
trailing after the full moon.

— *Kathryn Stripling Byer*

WILDWOOD FLOWER

I hoe thawed ground
with a vengeance. Winter has left
my house empty of dried beans
and meat. I am hungry

and now that a few buds appear
on the sycamore, I watch the road
winding down this dark mountain
not even the mule can climb
without a struggle. Long daylight

and nobody comes while my husband
traps rabbits, chops firewood, or
walks away into the thicket. Abandoned
to hoot owls and copperheads,

I begin to fear sickness. I wait
for pneumonia and lockjaw. Each month
I brew squaw tea for pain.
In the stream where I scrub my own blood
from rags, I can see all things flow
down from me into the valley.

Once I climbed the ridge
to the place where the sky
comes. Beyond me the mountains continued
like God. Is there no place to hide
from His silence? A woman must work

else she thinks too much. I hoe
this earth until I think of nothing
but the beans I will string,
the sweet corn I will grind into meal.

We must eat. I will learn
to be grateful for whatever comes to me.

— *Kathryn Stripling Byer*

MOUNTAIN PEOPLE

Mountain people
can't read,
can't write,
don't wear shoes,
don't have teeth,
don't use soap,
and don't talk plain.
They beat their kids,
beat their friends,
beat their neighbors,
and beat their dogs.
They live on cow peas,
fat back,
and twenty acres, straight up and down.
They don't have money.
They do have
fleas,
overalls,
tobacco patches,
shacks,

shot guns,
foodstamps,
liquor stills
and at least six junk cars in the front yard.
Right?
Well, let me tell you:
I'm from here,
I'm not like that,
and I am damned tired of being told I am.

— *Jo Carson*

I WROTE AND I WROTE

spent fortunes on notebooks
but they were not enough.
I wrote on the walls
of every building of every city
in the world. I wrote my name.
I wrote PICKLE WAS HERE,
PETER LOVES JOAN,
CALL THIS NUMBER FOR A GOOD TIME.
I wrote on the sidewalks,
on the streets.
YIELD AHEAD, I said, or STOP.
I organized the crowds
at football games to hold up cards.
GO COWBOYS! or GO DOLPHINS!
or BEAT THE BLUES! People thought
they were showing team support
but not so. I did it,
it was me, I wrote that too.

I tried all possible combinations
of words, every two in the language
that could be put together,
every three, four, five and more:
PEPSI SAYS WELCOME TO UPPER EAST
TENNESSEE!
GOD IS MY CO-PILOT!
MARTIN GUITARS ARE FINGER PICKIN' GOOD!
I wrote SURRENDER DOROTHY in the sky
I wrote in the Pharaoh's tombs
incantations to the sun.
I wrote on billboards and barnroofs.
BRING YOUR CAMERA TO ROCK CITY
I carved words on trees.
D. BOONE KILED BAR
I left memorandums buried in the ground
to be unearthed at the tri-centennial.
I wrote the Magna Carta
a magnum opus or two
and the Congressional Record.
I wrote letters home to mother
sad songs and erotic limericks
I wrote directions and confessions
recipes and treatises
documentaries and dissertations
tracts and tributes, trial and error.
I wrote the book.
I wrote my fingers to the bone.
I wrote up on the wrong side of the bed.
I wrote it off and I wrote the poem

but I am still searching for the words.

— *Jo Carson*

OLD-TIMER TO GRANDCHILD

And so our kinfolks let themselves
be sweet-talked into believing
that things would be the same.
They let some Philadelphia lawyers
tell them they could sell the yoke
and keep the egg, and with that few cents
they built a room onto the house
or somesuch. And now the yoke owners
are claiming their gold, and squashing
the shell and letting it fall howsumever
it falls. Let folks talk about our
backward ways. I like it. If forward's
what's been coming in right here lately,
I'd go into backup if I could. Back up
to the little creeks with fish in them,
the trees with birds, the caves with
animals, the air clean and smelling
of hay and apples. If forward's now,
then I feel sorry for the ones who'll
never know. But you will remember
a little bit. You tell them birds
do fly low before a storm.

— *Lillie D. Chaffin*

MEMORIAL TO ONE YEAR'S ABSENCE
for Cara

Wind catches in the Dutch Boy shutters;
shadows of Venetian blinds are rows
of dark robed mourners
on this indoor-outdoor carpeting.
Most coal miners are leaving their
daily interment,
are blinking at the brilliance
of late-day sun, honking
clear paths toward homes.
You close the shades on your aloneness,
deny this shift has ended, place
a Chinese poet, in translation, on
the extra pillow and lie beside it,
thinking the mattress and pillow
still hold his imprint.
Everything you need is here,
you tell the insurance-glass, sloshing
a wee-bit over—you and the glass.

— *Lillie D. Chaffin*

MY GRANDMOTHER WASHES HER VESSELS

In the white-washed medical-smelling milkhouse
She wrestled clanging steel; grumbled and trembled,
Hoisting the twenty-gallon cans to the ledge
Of the spring-run (six by three, a concrete grave
Of slow water). Before she toppled them in—
Dented armored soldiers booming in pain—
She stopped to rest, brushing a streak of damp
Hair back, white as underbark. She sighed.

"I ain't strong enough no more to heft these things.
I could now and then wish for a man
Or two. . . Or maybe not. More trouble, likely,
Than what their rations will get them to do."

The August six-o'clock sunlight struck a wry
Oblong on the north wall. Yellow light entering
This bone-white milkhouse recharged itself white,
Seeped pristine into the dozen strainer cloths
Drying overhead.

> "Don't you like men?"

Her hand hid the corner of her childlike grin
Where she'd dropped her upper plate and left a gap.
"Depends on the use you want them for," she said.
"Some things they're good at, some they oughtn't touch."

"Wasn't Grandaddy a good carpenter?"

She nodded absentminded. "He was fine.
Built churches, houses, barns in seven counties.
Built the old trout hatchery on Balsam. . .
Here. Give me a hand."

         We lifted down
Gently a can and held it till it drowned.
Gushed out of its headless neck a musky clabber
Whitening water like a bedsheet ghost.
I thought, Here spills the soldier's spirit out;
If I could drink a sip I'd know excitements
He has known; travails, battles, tourneys,
A short life fluttering with pennants.

         She grabbed
A frazzly long-handled brush and scrubbed his innards
Out. Dun flakes of dried milk floated up.
Streamed drainward. In his trachea water sucked
Obscenely, graying like a storm-sky.

"You never told me how you met."

         She straightened,
Rubbed the base of her spine with a dripping hand.
"Can't recollect. Some things, you know, just seem
To go clear from your mind. Probably
He spotted me at prayer meeting, or it could
Have been a barn-raising. That was the way
We did things then. Not like now, with the men
All hours cavorting up and down in cars."

Again she smiled. I might have sworn she winked.

"But what do you remember?"

46

"Oh, lots of things.
About all an old woman is good for
Is remembering. . . But getting married to Frank
Wasn't the beginning of my life.
I'd taught school up Greasy Branch since I
Was seventeen. And I took the first census
Ever in Madison County. You can't see
It now, but there was a flock of young men come
Knocking on my door. If I'd a mind
I could have danced six nights of the week."

We tugged the cleaned can out, upended it
To dry on the worn oak ledge, and pushed the other
Belching in. Slowly it filled and sank.

"Of course, it wasn't hard to pick Frank out,
The straightest-standing man I ever saw.
Had a waxed moustache and a chestnut mare.
Before I'd give my say I made him cut
That moustache off. I didn't relish kissing
A briar patch. He laughed when I said that,
Went home and shaved. . . It wasn't the picking and saying
That caused me to ponder, though. Getting married—
In church—in front of people—for good and all:
It makes you pause. Here I was twenty-eight,
Strong and healthy, not one day sick since I
Was born. What cause would I have to be waiting
On a man?"

Suddenly she sat on the spring-run edge
And stared bewildered at empty air, murmuring.
"I never said this to a soul, I don't
Know why . . . I told my papa, 'Please hitch me
The buggy Sunday noon. I can drive

Myself to my own wedding.' That's what I did,
I drove myself. A clear June day as cool
As April, and I came to where we used to ford
Laurel River a little above Coleman's mill,
And I stopped the horse and I thought and thought,
If I cross this river I won't turn back. I'll join
To that blue-eyed man as long as I've got breath.
There won't be nothing I can feel alone
About again. My heart came to my throat.
I suppose I must have wept. And then I heard
A yellowhammer in a willow tree
Just singing out, ringing like a dance-fiddle
Over the gurgly river-sound, just singing
To make the whole world hush to listen to him.
And then my tears stopped dropping down, and I touched
Nellie with the whip, and we crossed over."

— *Fred Chappell*

THE MAN OF STONES

my father wrote a poem forty years ago
    about laying stones for a wall
i found it when i was yet too young
    to decipher the lost tongue
        of this man's extinct hope;
he was a stranger on summer porches
    singing in a tender voice i never recognized,
        shadows coursed like poison streams
        down the deep furrows time had plowed
        from his nostrils to his dour mouth
i knew if my mother would take the hatchet

from the pickled bean shelf in the cellar
and strike his breast the steel
would ring upon solid rock,
i have read his statement of stoning
a hundred times since childhood
he moves now through dust-laden still life
a lone grey figure with the pervasive odor
of stale anger and aged bitterness
like vinegar gone flat
we do not speak of songs he sings no more
we seldom speak; but in the vacuum
i often hear the undeniable
crumble and groan
of old stones shifting.

— *Mary Joan Coleman*

FLOYD COLEMAN, MY GRANDFATHER

He was rocking
the thump of the homemade poplar rocker
shook the Tug River shack
which waded water on stilts
He was rocking
his right side dangled like a slack scarecrow
where the kettlebottom caught him
in the roof fall at the Lex mine
His voice was like the rush of raw water
down the Floyd County Kentucky hillside
where he picked the banjo when he was
young
and sang sassafras ballads and alum blues

Night and day he screamed out wild poems
which grew inside him like tangled thickets
            of bitter rooted mountain laurel
Shut up in Spencer State Asylum in 1925
            they never sent the body home
            said he died of natural causes
He was rocking
            the thump of that rocker is still shaking
            the foundations of my deep shafted heritage
And I say it is unnatural
            for a man to die
            from wanting so much to sing again.

— *Mary Joan Coleman*

DRIVING THE GAULEY RIVER, LISTENING TO THE RADIO

From the road I see King Coal has sprinkled down
his favors—new jeeps, wives on riding mowers,
remodelings, additions, and fresh paint.

This is a tale out of time.
Set it in these hills, in hard times.
Say she walked home in late November rain—
caught cold, of course. It ran to pneumonia.
Drowning, the doctor said, lungs filling with the dank
that settles in these mountain hollows.

The Preacher, the gathered kin, sang the grim
songs of sweet solemn hope, crossing over
to tarry on that brighter shore.

Her blue eyes clouded, she squeezed their hands,
saying, give Sis my best dress,
Cletus my 4th grade speller.
Said it like she had it by rote,
like it came to her from a country song.

And those anvil faces, that circle of skulls, sang,
rising toward a light they saw above
their shrouded hills. And every year they ran
her picture in the county paper—a small girl
with receding chin, limp hair, and bad teeth.

And the tale became a song.
It's maudlin, but I sing along, follow
the voices on my radio,
caught on the brambles of that twang,
hooked on the briars of her blue, blue eyes.

I drive beside the green river,
pulled curve by curve into the trees—
my own voice rising in terrible joy,
held in the circle of her thin arms,
certain she is asleep in Jesus.

— *Mark DeFoe*

BROWSING A BOOKSTORE IN APPALACHIA

Inside,
> through acres of pages
> parting the leaves—
> on this white ambience, the dark growth of words.

In a book of Zen I read:
> "The herons, riding the Spring wind,
> flap up from the Yangtze.
> I watch them glide, settle,
> snow on the emerald paddies."

In another, a funeral photograph:
> "Crushed in a roof fall."
> His horseshoe of mountain kin
> surround the bier.
> His older children, touching the coffin, pose.
> The smallest, with a face like a crushed peony,
> looks down at his father's hands,
> encased in the chalky gloves.

Outside,
> in wet cool clean air.
> Beneath an apple tree, in West Virginia,
> maroon paint on the hood of a pick-up
> floats trembling beads of mist,
> in each bead a confetti of blossoms.

I read

the message drifting there—
more petals, the wind says,
shifting massy folds of green,
and on the great wings of the hills the wind repeats,
more petals, more pink-white petals.

— *Mark DeFoe*

I HEAR HER SCREAM WHEN I SHOWER

I hear her scream when I shower
and when I saw in the basement
and when I cut the grass.
Her tiny cries come from the nozzle and the
        shower curtain and the tub
and from the gnawed wood
and from the explosions in the lawn mower.

I stop
and there's no sound
I start
the cries begin
but she's not crying is she?
crazy crazy
crying until I walk delirious through corridors of
        pure noise
pure weeping like a great light at the end.

— *Victor Depta*

A NEIGHBOR

I married at sixteen to get away
from home. We had two girls right off. I tried
to kill myself. They found me in time, I guess
I didn't really want to. Tommy had
a good job, didn't get drunk too often, liked
to tinker with cars—I forget how many he's had.
After we had the boy, I said that was
enough, and he agreed. Then I found out
I was pregnant again, this had to be the last.
Tommy made me have my tubes tied, not that
I didn't want to, too, even if he
wouldn't let me get the cat fixed. We're crazy
about animals, cats, dogs, rabbits, even
snakes. Tommy took a turn for the worse after
the baby came, there he was under thirty
and tied down with four children, know
how he felt but he should have thought of that sooner.
He started drinking and running around, said
he wanted a divorce, he'd let me have the children.
I said no, he'd have to take them. Things
got better. He decided we could get
a divorce and still live together. That little
piece of paper wouldn't be there to drag
him down. I agreed. Our house payment
was reduced and we got food stamps.
He stayed there most of the time, but saw his girlfriend,
too. I couldn't count on him, he was worthless.
One night I had a date with someone else.
Tommy got drunk and pistol-whipped me, lucky
he didn't kill me. He was really sorry
when he sobered up, he's been better

ever since. The neighbors don't lend us things
any more, someone complained and now
we don't get welfare. Last week
Tommy bought himself a motorcycle.

— *David Dooley*

FUEL

The ridge looms
& fills the cove before evening.
In this blue clarity
lamplight sets the cabins adrift
along the creek.
The gnawed surface of the woodblock
floats above its widening pond of pale dust & chips.
Within the chainsaw's roar
there is a core of silence
casually measured
smooth as walnut
stacked for use.

— *George Ellison*

7 MARCH 77

Dear Lynn, we found today that you are dead of yr own hand
in that far place. We don't know what to say or think & so
I am writing this to you to let you know that our memories
are of form & movement before the sickness in another time.
Martha said they found you in the barn. That was a good
place. & the act was yrs. I wish these lines would make
a poem for you but the words slur in my eyes & there is
no music in the creek.

— *George Ellison*

HE IS DEAD TO THE HILLS HE LOVED

He is dead to the hills he loved.
They cannot call him back to life again.

But I remember him
when the fields are turned for planting.
When I hear silver winds of summer,
see woodsmoke in the fall of the year,
and wild geese honk south for winter.

And I remember him
when there is rain on Pine Mountain.
When foxfire lights up dead logs at night,
when his bees work in the red clover
and wind whispers in the corn.

    I remember . . .
the day after the night he died—
frost-white fodder in the shock,
sumac leaves red enough to bleed,
yellow dirt where we dug his grave.

He is dead to all he loved.
We cannot call him back to life again.

— *Sydney Farr*

TO JAMES PRICE

Oklahoma is good land also
For farming and there are deer
Muskrat, rabbit, possum, squirrel
Fish in the rust streams.
It is not what you left—
There are no mountains
And summer's breath is dry—
But you have slept with disaster
And now the sky
Lightens with stars.
In your baskets and packs,
On horseback and on foot
What stories burdened the transfer
To this exile, your children's home?
You seeded my father's face
The harried pulse of his heart
Stalking wilderness settlements
For all creatures except the dead
Fathering lawyers, teachers

Ministers, bureaucrats
State employees
In this state without a past

In the 1837 Cherokee Census
Your name appears
"James Price
"Weaver and spinner, reads English"
My great-grandfather whose English
Saved him nothing of the Long March
Across Tennessee and north
Through Kentucky in time
To winter in Illinois
Because of an order which also
Specified blankets
But failed to deliver them.
I cannot know whether
He also lost children
In that winter's influenza.

So we live in jobs and marriages
Like divers strung from the surface
Of light by cords of breath,
stroking the frail entanglement
Of success, the corroded cargo
Toward which we swim,
Chuckling all the while
An inane astronaut prose, at best
A memorized statement to
Good fortune.

—*Jeffrey Folks*

TO GARY

Before we drove off
my father told me
you'd been rodeoing
four summers and not
to take up with you,
not to believe
anything you said.
Dragging out old fence
the spring of rusted wire
still threw you
half on your side
like a stubborn range steer
coiled in your wide arms.
That bright morning I worked
alongside you, bundling
the brown wire into
awkward spirals.
Then at the trailer over
iced tea and a basketball game
on the Sony, I heard you were
losing your son,
your wife already settled
outside the wilderness of
heart's distance

— *Jeffrey Folks*

THE FIRE CHIEF

A strong back indeed
she seethed remembering
a wedding toast years ago/
how he thumbed her
like magazines on his lap
and his liquid flame
singed her cheek/
how she'd heard her own mother
smoulder like her rocker
damned to ashes because
it screeched once too often
in the room where the big stove
burnt any offering/
and then the way he'd whisked
the girls with great tin buckets
down to "call on Mr. Coal"
lying in the railroad yard/
and when the Ohio threatened
to run its banks
in shiny black boots
from the window he'd scowl/
she'd watch for the waters to rise
and him out there floating/
but not yet not un
til the girls leave home she'd thought
so she mopped the hall
where his tracks blackened
and knew herself spineless
while he smoked at the fire station
where men in hard blue coats
called him / captain.

— *Kitty Frazier*

DOGWOOD TREE

A death has begun in the family.
A low cloud edges across the yard.
Near the house the dogwood tree loosens
its remote white blooms.
The bracts hang backward, the way
torn skin floats on its hinge.

In a room my father strains
against the heavy air
in his chest. Each slow breath
draws his son, his daughters closer
like a string winding deep
into their lives.

All night the branches fill
with sleeping moths. Beside his bed
where I have stayed this long
I wait for the pieces to unfasten,
wings, tattered bodies to drift off.

— *Marita Garin*

CLIMBING TO LINVILLE FALLS

1

Air over the mountain rises
shaping itself into someone's dream

Beside the path
soft green thorns brush our skin
rhododendron twist toward light

in that cage
their branches locked

2

At the falls the children run
toward noise

their flat screams dim
against the torrent gathering
everything into itself

We climb the massive rocks
edges smoothed away
by the clear purpose
of water

3

If you could feel water
cutting through layers
leaving mark after mark

If your body were rock
and water could ridge your flesh
the way time has wrinkled this rock
into folds

you would close your eyes
Nothing else would matter

4

High on the trail
your husband and children call
empty voices drifting
among the hemlock props

You're not ready
to leave
Something waits for you here

where nothing holds back
and everything returns to itself

5

Near the falls eyes watch you
from inside rock
a shadow moving inside a shadow
snake or some thin thing
living in a hollow

In such darkness life begins
or ends
a sleep as deliberate
as earth turning to rock

Indifferent to your body
water churns over ledges

6

At night the stars
are tiny threads of light
knotted in place

Your family gathers on a hillside
around a cone of flame
You reach for them
Your hands are shadows

trying to touch them
the water water moves against rock.

— *Marita Garin*

FINAL STRENGTH

terminal body
pains and capsules
so many colors and shapes
don't ask how I am
if you don't want to hear
about my chest, my side
just hold my hand
let me feel you
otherwise
turn on the television

here
eat my dinner

the air is hard
too hard to breathe
it is night in a dark house
but the brightness
shines in
I can pass through the window

— *Sharon Ginsburg*

POETS OF DARKNESS

Make them poets of the darkness,
For they speak from black faces
Lapping the sounds like red tongued dogs
Hurried after water.
We have seen them
Hunkered in the guts of steel
And we have seen their mantrips of segmented
                                  rusting cars
Being sucked and swallowed by long black holes.

Yes, make them poets
Make them hands of fossil ferns,
Give them grips on black diamond pens,
Have them speak Paleozoic languages
Decoded from Rosettas made of coal.

Make them tell us
What it means to see into aeons
Where no man has seen.

— *James B. Goode*

COUPLE

Long ago she vacated the body left
in bed beside him. He kneads the woman
on the counterpane. Her duty is to be there,
and she is—slick minx at sixteen, her core
dead at twenty. The man remembers
a wireless tune and worries at her
like someone determined to bring music
from static. He dreams a pure melody
of enhancement as he turns the dials. . . .
Clearly a green light flickers in her eyes.

— *Pat Gray*

SNAG

When I slept in the creek
it was winter. Not a rock talked,
not a star turned.
I was alone with water,
watched and watching,
as I slept the long freeze out.
In the spring I turned
in my hammock of sand,
slung between shores
like a net,
and dipped my dark leg
to the bedrock,
stood fast against the flood.
In summer now, I rise
high above the water,
collecting land wrack and foam,

steering the creek to my left and my right,
arranging the shape
of this farm,
filling a slough,
making my place by degrees.

At night I cast terrible shadows,
and the ghosts of the drowned,
like birds clinging close to the trunk,
sneak silently down my black branches.

— *Richard Hague*

LESSON

Once, I lay down
on a hillside,
spread my arms and legs out,
closed my eyes,
and dreamed of falling
towards the sky.
But I was frightened,
and the clouds came up too fast,
making faces blank as god's.
I shouted, grabbed
a root.
The old woods closed
around me.

Later, it was darkness.
It was breathing everywhere.
I could smell its blood, its rich meat,
I could hear it stalking
through the tops of trees,
the branches rustling, falling.

When I woke up everything
was peaceful, and more true.
The morning thunder made me happy.
The water in the deep spring
at the bottom of the hill
was sweet, and tempted me to drink.
I swallowed crawfish and old leaves.
They stayed inside me,
taught me how to think.

— *Richard Hague*

UNTITLED

January sky like bedsheets
in a house long ago abandoned.
Days spent weeding through debris.
There's nothing new here.
It's easy to believe
there's nothing new here.
Nights spent without dreaming,
what's the use in dreaming
just to wake again to endless sky?

February snow like winter washing,
clouds hung up above to dry.
This night the moon shines full
and dreams come slipping down.

— *Pauletta Hansel*

FIRST CUTTING

Twenty long teeth
tine and draw
the sweet orchard
hair of June

rose brush edges the slope
thinly grassed
in timothy

a cut of iron rings,
sings against it, is found
head up in the last windrow

through weightless lark nests,
berry bramble,
black & rasp,
the bar cuts, slides

slake   slake
slakeslake
slake   slake

rattle and turn,
and rock, bump and
the square ponies trot,
new white in the drizzle

the old rake winding
and clanking its stiff mouth.

— *Marc Harshman*

WIRE WIZARD

Hello. . . Hello. . .
Is there anybody awake
out in that cactus country?
This be the Greybeard
from Eastern Kentucky,
that hillbilly state.
Arizona? Nevada?
Shake! Shake!

We're tryin to get your way
but with all this rain

the skips rollin off the eastern coast.
It's been pourin here all day.
It's glistenin on the trees,
rollin off the ground
and hangin to the wires.
This be the Greybeard
comin your way.
My ears are wet. Shake! Shake!

There's no way I can get out,
no way to go anywhere
till you honkers
stop keyin up on that gold coast,
that California coast.
Talk to us Kentuckians
or clear the channel.

This be the hillbilly from Eastern Kentucky
better known down this way
as the Greybeard, the Greybeard.
Flyin over these wires,
we can go anywhere
when the channels clear.
We're gonna back way down now.
We're gonna shut this box down,
sit back and listen
to this heavy rain,
to your voices runnin in the air.
Goodnight, you wire wizzards.
This be Kentucky 529,
out of this coal town
closin her down.

— *Vicky Hayes*

WONDER WOMEN

From the center room
a blue light flickers.
My daughters watch television.
They are bionic.
My merely human pen
merely records
while DINNA DINNAAAAAA
they open padlocks by the power of mind
disarm the killer with the most deadly of karate
turn truckloads of nitroglycerine from the precipice
and lasso submarines like ponies.

They'll move on to better stuff:
bend open the bars of the county jail
bend back the arm of Kissinger
beat the B-1 into a pile of plumbing.

You watch them.

— *Mike Henson*

SMALL TRAGEDIES IN CIVILIZED PLACES, PART TWO

It was in '73.
I had been busted for possessing
something I did not possess
and had spent the night in jail.
In the morning,
before they let me out,
I had to stand in line
and sign a paper
to get my belongings back.
In front of me in line
was an old man,
busted for drunk.
He was so old
he had almost no flesh
left.
His eyes were two marbles
in the middle of a face
like an empty paper bag.

They had to push him,
move him along.
He didn't seem to understand
what they wanted.
The cops gave him a pencil,
and his hands shook so hard
he couldn't sign his name.
He dropped the pencil twice.
I can't, he said, his voice
like tires skidding over gravel.
So they took
him back
to his cell.

74   — *Ira Herman*

RENDEZVOUS

3
months
it had been
since we'd seen
each other.
We were to meet
in Paris
on the corner of a street
called Rue Titon
at twelve o'clock
Christmas day.

It was raining.
I was wearing a false beard,
dark glasses,
and a derby hat.
She was waiting in the rain,
looking the wrong way down the street.
Once, she stood on her toes to see farther.
Her hair was shorter,
more curly.
I'd forgotten how
gracefully made
she was,
like the Eiffel Tower,
or a butterfly's wing.

I wanted to run
but kept the act nicely,
walking slowly,
bent over like an old man,
quietly up behind her.

Excuse me, I said
in passable French,
would you like some wine?
I pulled a bottle from my coat.
Mais oui, she said,
playing my game,
I have a room by the Seine
where it is always evening...

Later
we laughed so hard
we fell out of bed.

— *Ira Herman*

A WOMAN TOO BIG FOR HER HOUSE

She should have seen it coming.
Her swelled bones had ached for weeks.
For weeks her expanding size
Had mocked the t.v.'s minute wives.
Climbing from the bath that day
The once-sepulchral tub suddenly seemed
A mere overlarge shoe, parodying Cinderella.
The mirror that backed the door
Could barely contain her torso.
Her arms had grown off somewhere,
A place she couldn't see.
She fled the room, afraid,
Hoping there was still time.
But all she could think to do
Was turn off the half-cooked supper.

Away across the kitchen,
The stove collapsed under her hand.
It was too late now and, besides,
She was beginning to like it.
One gentle nudge and the ironing board
Sat in a snapped-spider tangle.

Lying in the living room,
The furniture tickled like crumbs.
She cooled in the haphazard rain
Her condensed breath made on the ceiling.
She saw that each of her fingers
Was as big as a half-grown child,
Armless, multiple-waisted, untellably unique.
And her knees were mazes of runnels
Infrequently leveled by landscapes of scars.
She smiled with benign compassion
At the stunted fastness of her toes;
This was her world now; she was its god.

Her husband would be surprised
At the isthmus of thigh
That claimed the picture window
Where he had loomed all those other evenings
His shadow drowning the lawn.
He might be frightened away:
Perhaps she would be lonely.

This was, if the house could hold her,
If there were any room left for loneliness
Now that she was so large.

— *Sherry Holstein*

THE LAST UNMINED VEIN

Now it's neither here nor there
to most folks
but then I've never figured myself
to be like many
much less most
I know what they do
no matter what they say
I know how they come
with trucks bigger than ary road
can hold
and drive her through yer yard
and right up on the porch
and park her next to yer rocking chair
and you ain't got a howdy-do
to say about it neither
once you put yer name
to that paper
that's it

Now my daddy and me
we used to dig a little coal
out of that vein across the bottom
Just a pick and shovel
and what could be wheelbarrowed
out of there
was all that was took
and didn't hurt nothing
and kept a fire real good
and that's it
but that ain't what they got in mind
They wanting to make steel in Ohio

turn on the lights in New York City
and heat houses in Detroit
Shoot — I don't know a soul
in the whole state of Michigan
but that ain't really it
It ain't my business what they do with it
but this farm and everything that's in it
is plenty my concern
and I know how they come
with their mouths full of promises
and leaving with every one
of your fields full of ruts
and the mud sliding down the hillside
right onto your back steps
and there ain't a creek left
what would hold a living thing
and that's it
and the money
just don't mean that much to me
I done seen all I need to see
about where that money goes
and what's got with it
Last thing this county needs
is another new mobile home
with a four-wheel drive truck
parked on a mudbank in front of it
and that's it
and not another thing to show
for where and what your mammy and pappy
and their mammy and pappy
not to mention your own self and family
always had

So when that man in his new suit
and smooth as silk talking
came to my door
I didn't even ask him in
Said I wasn't interested
He laughed and said he wasn't selling
Said I didn't figure I was either
and that was it
Of course, I know he'll be back
but probably after I'm dead and gone
and if the children want to be so foolish
as to put an end
to what came long before them
ain't nothing I can do about it then
but I been laying plans
to remind them
of what it's gonna cost them
I done got my marker
and laid out the lines for my grave
right smack in the middle
of that vein
They gonna have to chip out the coal 6 foot by 6
and then put her right back on top of me
and that will be the end of that

— *Lee Howard*

LIVING IN APPALACHIA

Green cloys.
Roots burrow humus
attach quickly and hold.
Sky and sun have nothing to
do with each other.
Growth is silent here,
smells of old mushrooms
and goes rotten.
I awake from sleep so deep
only curling fronded fingers
tell me where I've been.
My eyes are afflicted
from living in caverns
and urges that once carried me
have disappeared.
I'm left behind voicing murmurs,
lost in the distance.
I put my ear to the ground
and hear motion,
rhythms of the earth's belly
swollen with river.
Everything is wet—
the match I strike
sputters and goes out
before it glows.

— *Dolores Jacobs*

SPRING FEVER

Everyone told me it would be easy—
a woman gets up from my couch
strides to my bedroom   undresses
turns out the light and whispers my name
but since I am clumsy and prone to nosebleeds
I accidently elbow myself in the face
during our passion and nearly hemorrhage
she thinks I'm a hemophiliac
and leaves me for another woman

Even though it is spring I am confused
forsythia sending out its yellow tentacles
waving them wildly in my face
I interpret this as a sexual message
and head for a local bar
where I find you bending over a pool table
with feline skill and patience
this is not the first time I realized you were bendable
I saw you bending over the kitchen sink
I saw you bending over the engine of your car
once I even saw you bending over my bed
but that could be misinterpreted

You make an incredible shot in the corner pocket
and give me a wink   I think
or maybe there was something in your eye
I can't be certain   there are so many variables
and everyone told me it would be easy.

— David Jarvis

82

SNAPSHOTS

It is Thanksgiving
and I am suspicious
of the warm day.
Stepping out of the house
away from the soiled plates
and napkins
I adjust my eyes
from the sharp light
of the kitchen
The yard is colorless
I know it can't
possibly be dreaming
of June
This is only in me.

Around the yard—
I take old steps
I took as a child
My hands remember how
to grip a rusted
swing chain so it
doesn't pinch
or racing through clover
hoping this time
to avoid the sting.

Looking back toward the house
the windows glow
In one
I catch first
my sister
Then my grandmother

I listen to their silent conversation
in the overheated kitchen
They are posed in the illuminated
frames
These are the snapshots I want
to carry with me— smashed
in my wallet, stoic on my dusty
chest of drawers, obedient on my mantle.

Later
On the back steps
My sister and I drink coffee
from adult cups
We are embarrassed
We don't look into each other's eyes
We haven't played together for so many years
She knows we will never play again
The world has discovered us
It would never be the same.

— David Jarvis

THE KELLYS' REUNION

Stiff as starch, obviously ancestral,
Grandma and Pa Kelly stare
Out of the dark daguerreotype
All reverently pass.

Could they commence such straying flock?
Across church grounds, stranger-cousins
Gather at shady picnic tables, buzzing
Out of the heat, removing ties.

A tardy van pulls up, unloading
An aunt—oh really?—divorced, who totes
One more bucket of cold fried
Chicken, watery tea.

Uncle Brown, cornering his quarry,
Gestures with a drumstick. Cora
Spots Bett in an unfriendly crowd
Sipping the annual gossip.

A throat clears. Nominations
Are open for next year's officers.
Palms are lifted. Oscar, who only
Came to eat, is elected

President by acclamation.
He nods above his plate, accepting,
Elbowing his wadded napkin
Onto the Baptist grass.

An announcement. Talkers and eaters
Press together, bumping, posturing,
For the hired photographer.
All sizes, all ages, all smiles.

Grandma and Pa never blink.

— *Carey Jobe*

from MELVIN ISAACS

2

Once he heard geese in the night
and saw them black against full moon,
going far beyond the world he knew.
Once another year, he woke to honking
in a far cornfield,
and with fluttering chest
he stalked them on knees and belly,
saw them rise all in an instant,
felt his own trembling as he fired,
saw one spiral to earth, a lesser thing.
At once he mourned the fowl
and the death of innocence
and tried to imagine
the place of the goose's going.

7

"The house my grandfather built was by those
                              parked cars,"
he said, "And the meadow sloped there to a pond.
Woolworth's does business over the barn's
                              foundations.
I plowed the garden under Rexall's
and horses ran where the department store squats.
Progress had to come, they all said.
We must be served with transistors and
                              doubleknits.
They're dearer to us now, you know,
than dew on a meadow,
wind through a horse's mane
or green things sprouting from tended earth.
Progress is a fickle bitch," he said
toward the blue mountains.

86   — *Loyal Jones*

AMERICAN FOREST

Backside of nowhere, Alabama,
green sails of loblollies climb
out of ruts settlers made
going back home. Dying, my
grandfather showed me terraces
under tall trees, limestone
washed up like drowned sheep,
bushes wild haired as prophets
where well behaved crops had grown.
Trees he knew as well as settlers
who hung their names on coves
repossessed by glum storekeepers.
Those orphans of the forest
went ahead of us and behind us,
and for awhile, our lives were
those trees stopping at a clearing,
fenceposts split and greyed by snow,
the lattice-work of a well house
scrawled in hieroglyphs of kudzu,
and those two elderly lovers,
the chimneys, remembering the ashes
like a nightgown at their feet.
At a stump, we paused, considering
shade, then started back down
the mountain, guns on our shoulders.
Our steps make the deer invisible.

— *Rodney Jones*

DULCIMER

Out of chicory spliced in hedgerow,
Out of ramp and bitteroot, polk
And wood sorrel, from the old house
With two rooms, spreading newspapers
Against the cold, from bear tracks
In the lot, through the paralyzed light

Of barns coiled in privet, from spring
To river, firing white, rocking
For lowlands, your life comes,
Wherever it meant, becoming, to go,
To one string ringing over the body
Of a sleeping woman, her ribs

Stained from chestnut and sassafras,
The dark heart followed there,
And two strings asleep in the moon's
Icy briars, dripping on clematis
And stone, and the valley sleeping
Beside the mountain, its peaks

Great snow patches of blue
And cinquefoil, balsalm and rhododendron,
The farmer sleeping by the seamstress,
Two strings asleep, the other dreaming
In the perfect pitch of gospels, how
You heard the diamondback once, and knew.

— *Rodney Jones*

LIFE AND ART IN EAST TENNESSEE

I had read in National Geographic
how in Alaska, or some places like it
where chill mysteries winter,
people stand on ice ten months thick
and see fish glint far beneath
shivering the deep green with their speed.

I stood on creek ice
one windfall of a subzero day
skating thin and bladeless
on a dare. Dreaming of parkas,
the huskies' bark, a fish-hook gleaming
carved from a fat walrus tusk,
I saw only the bent brown ribs
of the old year's reeds
like a kayak skeleton
breaking up in the backwater.

Whatever I saw or didn't in the mud,
come spring and full summer
the creek overflowed
with tadpoles, snapping-turtles, water-bugs,
the green wink of a lizard disappearing.
I kept one eye peeled
in hopes of cottonmouth, water-moccasin
as I kneeled in the weeds, sleeve hiked,
feeling in water brown as tobacco
for the least thrill of minnows
shimmering between my fingers.

— *Jane Wilson Joyce*

RIVERS

The Legendary Dock Boggs
Up in Letcher County Kentucky sang

> O Death!
> Oo Dea—ee—aa—ee—ath
> Please spare me over for another year

And for a long time, Death did.
Spare him.
And then he didn't.
And I have seen the North Fork
Tug Fork
Poor Fork
The Cumberland
The green

> Ohio down to Cairo
> Straddle addle addle bobaladdle bobalinktum
> Rinktum boddy mitchy cambo

I have leaned out heart hurting over the Liffey,
                              the Shannon
And I have seen the *Tiber*
Walked beside the *very* Tiber!
And before me rockteetering
Nimble faunfeet first one then the other
Curleyheaded sweet faunfaced homesick husband
                              hollering singing

Seven long years I've been in prison
Seven or more I've got to stay
Just for knocking a man down in the alley
And taking his gold watch a-way

Ridiculous song to sing balancing by the very Tiber
A song of The Legendary Dock Boggs
Brought to Rome by this faunheaded TexasBaptist boy.
Nobody steps in the same river once.

— *Sheila Joyce*

HER WORDS

You gotta strap it on
she would say to me
there comes this hardship
an you gotta get on up the creek
—there's others besides you—
so you strap it on
Oh, you give St. Jude what he'll take
hand it over like persimmons
with the frost on
It aint nothin
There's more stones in that river
than you've stepped on
or are about to
Once your hands
can get around sumac
once your feet
know the lash of a snake

you'll strap it on
that's what a good neck
an shoulders are for

In winter
at the settlement school
our wet hair would freeze
on the sleepin porch
an we'd wake up
vain younguns that we were
under blankets of real snow
Come Christmas
we'd walk sixteen miles
home to Redbird mission
only once gettin
lost in the woods
snowed over
down the wrong ridge

Nobody's askin
for what aint been done—
build against cold
an death scalds the dark—
you strap it on
there's strength in the bindin
I scrubbed on a board
I know what it's about

— *George Ella Lyon*

HOW THE LETTERS BLOOM LIKE A CATALPA TREE

in this poem, on a day when tulip bells
ring up from the ground, when the crab apple
swarms with blossoms. How I would like
the words to shine always like sword grass
and be stubborn as thistle and come to you
heady as lilac, as dandelion to the new bee.

But you have read this
so many times, the message
patched and worn like sleeves.
You've seen words die
down, thought ravel
as green comes on
and flowers are forced
to the ground. And you've
seen farther: green grown
ragged, the words old wood
storms break against the house.
What could I send you?

On Cowan Creek in Letcher County, Oaksie Caudill
is making a white oak basket. He cuts down a tree,
peels and splits it, pressing, whittling the ribs.
No waste and no hurry. He's got time as much as time's
got him. He makes the frame: two hoops, braces, and a binding
which at the handle looks like the old God's Eye.
Oaksie's not above impure improvements—tape and wire
to hold him as he goes. Still, it's slow, worrisome;
sometimes a splint turns brittle, sometimes a loop
whips back and stings the eye. Body gets cramped,
muscles like staves in the basket, all their tension bent

on springing free. Oaksie walks out, chews a twist
of Red Man, sees how burdock came on past the snow.
But soon he's back, bent to his wood-weaving,
the half-globe between his bony knees.

Oaksie's trade is this translating
of straight to curve, of fact to what we need,
tough as a poem for the burden that outlasts us,
for a heart leafed with words like a tree.

— *George Ella Lyon*

FLORA

Husband killed by company mines,
evicted from company house,
Flora
shame-fled
by night
with her five children
out of the company town
            and into the ghetto.

On aching legs,
she laundered and ironed clothes.

In the winter,
sharing one pair of shoes,
brothers took turns
carrying brothers to school.
Then orphanages took the children,
            scattering the family.

94

On aching legs,
she laundered and ironed clothes.

A whorehouse madam
said she dreamt
an angel, glowing with light,
                                    crossed
                her porch.
From the angel,
glowing in the wood-worn steps
of wandering wineheads, strays, shy
hillbillies and reeling drunks,
told the madam to sell her house to
Flora
for half price and without a down payment,
so she could have a home for her family,
                and that
"She, the madam, was good."
And she sold her house to Flora.

And a fresh, clean smell
pushed out that
"odor indefinable, peculiar to all whorehouses"
aptly described by William Faulkner.
And crosses and pictures of saints
replaced
mirrors on the walls.

And the family did prosper.

— *Russell Marano*

THE BEGINNING
For Ian

You say the world is
always presenting possibilities.
I think: expansion. Contraction.
The way children are born.
Head first. Painful. So
what narrows us down? Is it
geography? The towns between
have only their names to
guide us. Minot. Oceola.

One night, standing on the
edge of the Great Plains, I
saw the wind bearing down. It
howled like the animal it is;
particle by particle, stripped
the car of paint, beat against
the windows of that wooden
house. By morning, it had
eaten down the grain of
the wood. I have forgotten
the name of that town. All
I remember is the wind
and its sharp, precise voice
that said: I eat the past
and move on.
The future follows just behind
that wind.

— *Adrianne Marcus*

IN A SOUTHERLY DIRECTION

It's just

over the knob

there —

you know the place,

the one

up there next to

Beulah Justice,

your mother's second cousin

on her daddy's side.

Or

if you go in by

the back road

it's the farm across the way

from Jesse's old barn

that burned down

last June

with them 2 fine mules

of his.

Why hell, son,

you can't miss it.

— *Jeff Daniel Marion*

EBBING & FLOWING SPRING

Coming back you almost
expect to find the dipper
gourd hung there by the latch.
Matilda always kept it hidden
inside the white-washed shed,
now a springhouse of the cool
darkness & two rusting milk cans.
"Dip and drink," she'd say,
"It's best when the water is rising."
A coldness slowly cradled
in the mottled gourd.
Hourly some secret clock
spilled its time in water,
rising momentarily only
to ebb back into trickle.
You waited while
Matilda's stories flowed back,
seeds & seasons, names & signs,
almanac of all her days.
How her great-great grandfather
claimed this land, gift
of a Cherokee chief
who called it "spring of many risings."
Moons & years & generations
& now Matilda alone.
You listen.
It's a quiet beginning
but before you know it
the water's up & around you
flowing by.
You reach for the dipper
that's gone, then

remember to use your hands
as a cup for the cold
that aches & lingers.
This is what you have come for.
Drink.

— *Jeff Daniel Marion*

JELLY BREAD

Mom would give my dad an extra jelly
sandwich in his lunch bucket so he could
bring it home for one of us kids. It would
be soft-damp and taste like it had soaked
the black out of the air, even through
waxed paper. I ate it trying not to taste
or feel anything but my dad's bringing me
something. When I got bigger, I tried not
to be around when he came home.

— *Margaret McDowell*

RECLAMATION

In a cornfield near Canton
by an easy bend of the lane-and-a-half blacktop
pebbled with the bed of the nearby Pigeon
leans an old drive-in movie screen.
Kudzu vines thread the braces
loose below and behind, buckling crazy
as the trellis some old lady
tacked on to the ticket booth seasons ago
when her boys took it for a tractor shed.
Panels warped and moonshot, like a drunk
checkerboard, the screen still
looks clear across the corrugated fence
into the next field, where cows cool
in the concession stand. In the shade
men sit on huge wooden spools
the phone company left behind, talking up
the loft, the other three walls
of the tallest barn in Madison County.

— *Michael McFee*

SIGNS AND WONDERS

Except ye see signs and wonders,
ye will not believe

1.
ECLECTIC BEVERAGE BOARD
AT A TASTEE FREEZE
IN DILLWYN, VIRGINIA

Drinks:
Coca-Cola
Dr. Pepper
Sprite
Orange
Fish
Coffee

2.
WEATHERED INSINUATION
OVER A COUNTRY-STORE-CUM-SERVICE-STATION
ON THE ROAD TO CAROLINA BEACH

Notions
and
Lubrication

— *Michael McFee*

LEGACY'S DAUGHTER

Old white
liberal—
I know your mind
like the veins
in my hand. Twisting
tortuous
red & blue
whipping like banners in the wind
—they all run back
to the heart
your old, white heart.

Your fingers
gnarl a pencil
while your brain cells
trace over the same dark bundles of five
marking time.
Nothing happens
after the fall of Normandy.
The Twentieth Century ends
with FDR.
All's well that ends well
You remember the middle names
of every GI in Company C
Some did not return. You keep them locked
alive
in your brain cells
swimming in your synapses
searching for a beach head   sinking   sinking
1946 and the whole damn country turned to sand.

— *Bonni McKeown*

MOTHER MILKING
for Christene McKinnie

Turn down the brim of your old felt hat
so all I can see are your rosy lips

Chew on them absently
Think thoughts I have no way of hearing

Step carefully through
the muck of the barn

Stop to look at the beginning of sun:
beside each brown slat a blue one

Sigh and rub the ache in the bone
the place over the heart where fullness

has flown like a hen out of a coop   go
around the black snake that lies in your path

The eggs inside its belly strung out
like cocoons just before the butterflies

emerge from their safekeeping   Shush the hens
that roost in a row on the cow's back

Listen to the soft cooing issuing
from their throats to the ruffling

of their shiny feathers as they rise
to the rafters like powder puffs

Here where nothing moves but the cow chewing
its cud   its dull stare turning to rock

Make your hands flash in the dark
make them light up the barn

as they take me back to that moment
in my childhood where nothing belongs but milk

filling the pail inch by inch
with its white froth

warm and sweet
as the breath of a baby

— *Llewellyn McKernan*

FOSSIL FUEL

Mostly I wake up because I am crowded
by little hairs
by gases underground
by the necessity to be polite
even in sleep
by a song over and over
because I am too hot
and would rather lie flat

and the pillows are rocks under my head
because I have not written anything
because a friend maneuvered me
   into washing the dishes
   and it's his house
because you will wake up and ask why I am awake
and not want to know
but I will be burning to tell
I can't digest anything properly
the desire to please
is stark as death
oh yes/I said to the vet
I'll wait/excuse this delicate
dying animal yes
   she who had waited two days lost in the long grass
tea?
for the undertaker
   the flowers of my mother's china broke and wept
you were a prospector?
I play these tidbits to the hilt
how interesting! imagine!

O empathy impedes
and pleasing bleeds
and here in the night I lie
steamy and dangerous, the press of my crushed ferns
making charcoal
I will burn slowly in this bed I have made have made
   for a long time.

— *Devon McNamara*

THE NEW CORBIES

If trees remain and carrion crows
Still gather on the oak,
That morning when the green wind blows
And carries off the smoke,
The crows will find below them there,
All blooming from the ground,
As flowered and as fat a feast
As crows have ever found.

Of scarlet red and bloated white,
And flowered full in bloom
Those tropic blossoms all will burst
To waft their sweet perfume.

And floating from the oak tree's limb,
Like hunger, then the crows
Will taste of man and savor him—
The richest fruit that grows,
When from the forehead of his dream
Exudes the atom rose.

— *Louise McNeill*

OLD BODINE CROW

Bodine Crow see-sawed on the schoolhouse well-sweep
And did other ornery things
That good children didn't do.

He'd talk to the store-keeper with his right hand
And steal with his left, a passel of times.

When he growed up he hid his likker in a holler tree
And when he seen the sheriff comin'
He jumped in with it,
And liked never to've got back out.

'Fore he got clear old
Somebody shot him.
Like ever'body else he died,
Only a little sooner,
Sorry thing.

— *Alice McNew*

ON MEETING FERLINGHETTI'S MORTICIAN

A funeral home is a funny place
                  when you're six years old
  and wear braids
          tied with green and white
                    polka-dotted ribbons
I mean people cry a lot
        and stuff
             but still
      it's kinda funny
         when you're six
and your Daddy
      wears a long white coat
           and squeaky gloves
              and smells like fluid

       when you're six
          people always look so sad and scared
        standing in the entryway
             but upstairs
    you have to giggle a little
       jumping across the open landing
          without your bathrobe

I mean
      when you're six
and you've always lived
         with death
    yes I guess
      a funeral home is a funny place
  until one day
      you cut off your braids
      and read that

the same guy
>you used to sneak up on
>>in his sleepy brown recliner
>and pull a toothpick from his mouth
Is Ferlinghetti's smiling
>>mortician
>waiting with eager hands

Somehow it's easier
>to laugh
when you're six

>*— Evelyn Miller*

THE VINEGAR JUG

It's on account of you,
I start the day off drinking,
sucking my bitter sop,
preening pretty fur.

I might tame a wild animal
to appreciate me,
to lick my paw, gaze at me with sweet dull eyes.
But I might never clear the land—as you have done—
of beasts and creeping things,
make it safe,
squeeze its wine
in the right wine-season.

These are the shining chains
you make for me.
A man and his wife living in a vinegar jug,
and they were happy.
He sang to her some songs,
each note dying and reforming
in its brother.

At night she rubbed her feet,
smiling at the gold shackle
around the petty bone.

— *Heather Ross Miller*

LUMBEE CHILDREN

They are like figurines.

I am in the presence of relics,
treasures from the Inca pyramids.
So I tote the sight of them
like bright jewels
in my uneasy mind.

Their names come across the desk,
dull, tame as any enlisted English muster.
I hope for one Standing Bear among them,
one Cochise,
one dazzling Coyote-Man.
They don't give me any.

Not a feather, a bead,
not a string,
not one ragged buckskin.
They came out of the pyramids
no older than the day
they went in.

I want to arm them,
give them the bow, the fancy repeating rifle,
the beautiful bomb.
They should have it.

But these are figurines,
turning in the sun,
feeding that ancient uneasy star.
Somewhere,
the priest in the pyramid
has already raised the knife.

— *Heather Ross Miller*

THE BRIER LOSING TOUCH WITH HIS TRADITIONS

Once he was a chairmaker
People up north discovered him.
They said he was "an authentic mountain craftsman."
People came and made pictures of him working,
wrote him up in the newspapers.

He got famous.
Got a lot of orders for his chairs.

When he moved up to Cincinnati
so he could be closer to his market
(besides, a lot of his people lived there now)
he found out he was a Brier.

And when his customers found out
he was using an electric lathe and power drill
just to keep up with all the orders,
they said he was losing touch with his traditions.
His orders fell off something awful.
He figured it had been a bad mistake
to let the magazine people take those pictures
of him with his power tools, clean-shaven,
wearing a flowered sport shirt and drip-dry pants.

So he moved back down to east Kentucky.
Had himself a brochure printed up
with a picture of him using his hand lathe,
bearded, barefoot, in faded overalls.
Then when folks would come from the magazines,
he'd get rid of them before suppertime
so he could put on his shoes, his flowered sport shirt
and double-knit pants, and open a can of beer
and watch the six-thirty news on tv
out of New York and Washington.

He had to have some time to be himself.

— *Jim Wayne Miller*

LIVING WITH CHILDREN

Sorcerers, they've turned
the house into a serialized fairy tale.
The plot, full of reversals,
mysterious messages, unfolds
day after day, surprising
as fried marbles underfoot.

A frog on the floor, waiting to be kissed.
A rabbit, a pet snake.
Half a sandwich shelved with books.
Ghosts, guns, flowers.
Winged, web-footed snakes drawn
on the walls of bedrooms, their caves.

There is an enchanted forest inhabited
by crayola people who fear
the heat of the sun and never venture
from under their crayola trees—so different

from the watercolor folk, who live
in an eternal spring, standing forever
in watercolor puddles, hands reaching up
to a sun that looks down on them,
a blissful idiot.

In my desk drawer, an unfamiliar
piece of paper that accordions out:
"Don't touch this or you'll die!"

It's too late.

—*Jim Wayne Miller*

AN OLD STORY—RETOLD

Gretel
there are
no bread crumbs
to lead
you back
but you keep
looking
for some sure guide
some
line
to catch
hold of
to lead
you through
your black forest
stop crawling
and
look up Gretel
see
the birds fly dark
against
a cold white moon
their stomachs full
of your damn
bread crumbs.

— *Elizabeth Moore*

THE WAY BACK

The mountains are barren
in the season
you would have been born,

their useless bellies push
against Christmas sky.

It is the month of children
like those on the doctor's
bulletin board
in the room where he put me,

the one time I have ever lain
in that room,

his affirmation, "You have
certainly had a miscarriage"
attached to my
long night of losing.

A difficult way to daylight
it comes. I find it months later,
kneading dough for a seasonal bread,
the first I have ever made,
awaiting its rise in the oven.

— *Janice Townley Moore*

CHAD

when the little boy

with eyes full of sparrows

died

I threw away my bells
and let my candles burn to
nothing

and imagined
the drunk driver
sitting in a silo
sucking his thumb

but the little boy

with bones light as hay

offers his blanket
to the man
in the silo
and whistles the air
in red backyard
swings

and the little boy

with tapers for fingers

is lighting my bones.

— *Maureen Morehead*

AND ALL THOSE NAKED MEN

About this place,
Or any such similar one,
I suppose most people
Hold memories of the pounding surf,
Oysters Rockefeller, fireworks on the Fourth,
Or Guy Lombardo and his Royal Canadians;
But what I'm able to pull up
Through all these intervening years
Is a certain room with certain features:
   Wooden benches,
   A slippery grating on the floor,
   The light filtering through the louvers,
   Unsure laughter in the shower,
   The smell of moist towels,
And having to take my own pants down
In front of dad and all those naked men.

— *Allan Morgan*

CANNING TIME

The floor was muddy with the juice of peaches
and my mother's thumb, bandaged for the slicing,
watersobbed. She and Aunt Wessie skinned
bushels that day, fat Georgia Belles
slit streaming into the pot. Their knives
paid out limp bands onto the heap
of parings. It took care to pack the jars,
reaching in to stack the halves
firm without bruising, and lowering
the heavy racks into the boiler already

trembling with steam, the stove malignant
in heat. As Wessie wiped her face
the kitchen sweated its sweet filth.
In that hell they sealed the quickly browning
flesh in capsules of honey, making crystals
of separate air across the vacuums.
The heat and pressure were enough to grow
diamonds as they measured hot
syrup into quarts. By supper the last jar
was set on the counter to cool
into isolation. Later in the night
each little urn would pop as it
achieved its private atmosphere and
we cooled into sleep, the stove now
neutral. The stones already
pecked clean in the yard were free to try
again for the sun. The orchard meat fixed in
cells would be taken down cellar in the
morning to stay gold like specimens
set out and labelled, a vegetal
battery we'd hook up later. The women
too tired to rest easily think of
the treasure they've laid up today
for preservation at coffin level, down there
where moth and rust and worms corrupt,
a first foundation of shells to be
fired at the winter's muddy back.

— *Robert Morgan*

CHESTNUT

Opening a chestnut we find a huge eye
staring between whiskered lids.
This animal gone to extinction left
its eyes to remind us
we're being watched
through the earth's dark lens.

— *Robert Morgan*

THE ENGAGEMENT

This is how it starts:
to entertain
your newly married friends have
asked you over.
You're expected
to show.

They answer the door like Siamese twins;
they look at you
as though you were a salesman.
Half smiling,
you enter their home
like a foot in a tight shoe.

You get the guided tour,
from bedroom satin
to bathroom porcelain.
You are moved.
They are pleased.
All sit down.

Their furniture is new;
wherever you sit
you draw their attention like a stain.

Across from you, they sit
in the love seat.
They kiss each other's cheek
whenever it's in range.
You observe at a distance,
expressionless as a clock,
pretending to make time
with your hands.

They ask you how you do it
alone.
You're tempted to show them
dance lesson receipts,
movie ticket stubs,
bar tabs,
canceled checks,
but, instead, you ask them
only to remember.

When you start feeling
like an orphan,
it's time to go.
They say, Too soon,
stay and watch the late show -
but you're no voyeur;
you bow out
with a nun's grace.
Perfect hosts,

they tell you to come back, soon,
to bring someone
(as though you were a ventriloquist).

By the way,
there's no ending
to this;
with practice,
you merely get better.

— *Donald Narkevic*

TRAIN HORN

The L & N shoves a load of coal
into the Black Mountain night
and Poor Fork fights the sounds
of train horns by carving stillness
and washing noises down toward Harlan.

Must be the click of wheels
and echoes cushioned in
mountain squeezed valleys
that make old men and old women
and young boys and girls perk ears
when train horns blow.

I have seen them down at the crossing,
their eyes dug out with silence,
their mouths hanging caves on faces
and their feet tapping rhythm of train horn blow.

— *Lee Pennington*

DISCOVERED

A skinny girl with cornstalk legs
And hair like straw
Was mocked by her classmates
For her Goodwill clothes
And self-pitying seriousness.

While they attended ballgames
And worshipped Max Factor,
She hid safely in her room
Reading big thick books
Full of philosophical questions,
And very small print:
Kant, Freud, Camus
She still didn't understand
While the flames licked the posters off the wall
And the rug grew too warm for her feet.

At 16, she begged with adolescent fervor for
        THE ANSWER
Till one Sunday afternoon, the air wet with tears
She said no to the easiest one.

It's a good thing.

For a curly haired boy in overalls
With cat-grey eyes
And a Wonderfully Hard Body
Discovered her
Introduced her to the joy of unreserved excess
To a different kind of flames

And convinced her
That it was not up to the 16-year-olds of the world
To answer the question.

— *Rita Quillen*

THE JOYS OF HOUSE WRECKING

Builders are a sorry lot.
They start low, they follow rules.
Wreckers start at the top.

Unroofing under the sun,
releasing prisoner nails
to the society of grass below,
flying frisbee shingles some drudge lugged up
to random lodging in the kudzu's throat.

Like those ten-year-old surgeons,
rubber-gloved and skittish
behind the shadowing sheet,
who lift to the joy of friends assembled
all manner of junk from the patient's gullet or gut—
sausages, a mop, old swords, or a large fish—
I strip away sheathing and haul from the attic
all unretrieved shards, hulks, husks,
the comic bones of incompetent beds, raggedy rags,
a grey mattress brain with a low I.Q.
All turn in the air,
all fall down.
Gravity plays my game.

Now ceiling bone connected to de. . .wall bone,
Wall bone connected to de. . .floor bone,
Now hear de word of de. . .
Wrecking bar.
It talks loud, it talks the house down
in a big lovely hurry of plaster and soot.

Liberate that lath! Hoist a joist!
Free that window! It's been framed.

In my joy under the sun,
I follow the head of my 8-pound sledge,
I follow no rule but the rule of break,
bury the bits in the cellar,
turn back time to a zero house.

I sing in the sun and wind and wonder
how God can wait.

— *Larry Richman*

SPRING LEAFFALL

For my daughter and me
there is no sleeping late.
We look out her window
at the woods: against
the gray geometry of trees
there are purple smudges,
and at the tops
faint yellow stains.

The wind comes up.
Errant leaves
shatter from branches
like drunken birds.
They have spent the winter
holding on, tatters of brown paper,
tough as old folks in a nursinghome,
only to fall among the redbud blossoms,
out of season, upon the warming ground.

— *Anne Roney*

GIFT CARD

Dear Mother
I know I was the child
you didn't want.
Daddy told me how
he sweet-talked you
that night in Memphis
because he wanted a girl.
There you were, just getting
the last boy off to school
and pregnant.
You sent messages through the cord
you owe me... you owe me

I think it was bearable ten years or so
till you wished your mother dead
and she died in mid-sentence
hand in the air
and you saw sudden lumps
under my T-shirt.

I didn't even know you were sick
when you began the rounds
of genteel hospitals
under a variety of pseudonyms
for hatred, anger, and lust.
You wired the shocks right back to me,
the messages were all the same.

For fifty years you have
smiled over the payments
and never issued a receipt
nor crossed out a debt.

By the time you receive this box
I will be gone.
Open it with care, the
jar is made of crystal,
the better for you to see
my fist-sized bloodred womb,
this, the last present to show
you once had,
very truly yours,
A Daughter.

— *Anne Roney*

AFTERNOON AT THE SPORTSMAN

They seldom look for gold anymore
the old men, for here in the mountains
they have found a quieter time,
a wooden womb of smoke and dust.

They have become transfixed in a world
of fifteen-cent beers and hand rolled
cigarettes.

The young men too flock here, reading
the marvelous tales of the old men like
holy braille. And vowing that someday
they too will find the precious metal.

This is an elegant threshold, where life
is reduced to its lowest common denominator.

Bragging and betting, young men hover
above the velvet plane where they find that
like their sad wives, even ivory deceives
them.

And old men, still cooling their threats,
slowly cast their gaze into a room
they left years ago.

— *John Russell*

THE PORCH AND THE SYCAMORE

The porch is so near
the sycamore
its paint peels
exactly like bark.

I don't understand
why the porch has no steps
but the tree has five
spiked to it.

It's got something to do
with the porch being stuck
high on the back of the house
and sagging with its own weight

while the tree grows and grows.
Whoever lived here before me
wanted to cut the tree
but propped the porch up.

If I could graft the porch
to the sycamore
I'd forget about paint
and sit in the tree.

— *Timothy Russell*

BLUEGRASS INTERVAL

Because I got away from you,
sat the afternoon by Nottely River,
chilling my toes with three small boys
slim as minnows in brown water;

feasted on bluegrass sounds,
a dulcimer and two guitars
keening in the breeze of an oak;

tasted the bitterness of walnuts
in home-made brownies sold at a booth,
with coffee sweet in a plastic cup,

punish me.
I could have stayed at home
and listened to your breath
rasping in the shuttered room
like a warped guitar.

— *Bettie Sellers*

MYCENAE

Wild poppies scatter fresh drops
of ancient blood, red across the hill
beehived with Agamemnon's tomb.
Sparrows nest between the stones,
twittering as though the years
were few since Clytemnestra stood
waiting for a flame on Ida's peak.
Guides sketch a triangle of lions,
keystone for a city gate,
and dusty tourists press against
Mycenae's walls, shading their faces
from the merciless eye of God.

— *Bettie Sellers*

MA RAN AND HID IN THE SMOKEHOUSE

Ma ran and hid in the smokehouse
    they said
    when mother was ready to leave to get married
    a Gabbard boy from Indian Creek
    she'd got up with at teachers college
Wouldn't come out to tell them good-bye
nor let anybody else in the smokehouse either
    Pa said
till way past time to start supper.

And forty years later this morning, you
turning me back at the corner
of adolescence and New Circle Road
rather

you said
go the rest of the way alone
left me
fanned sick by passing cars
standing there feeling
watching you turn and wave and turn
again
and walk across the curve of the world
toward Winburn Junior High.

— *Anne Shelby*

SONG FROM THE DISTANT NATIVE

I look at my legs   long and lean
like silken milk poured
in thin streams   from an ivory pitcher.
As pale as two distant moons
that are aloof yet full with light.
Then I think,
just a tint, with a brown that begins
like a deep cloud that passes the face
of the moon shades it
makes us search for it
find its shine beneath
then I think,
just one shade more
to bring out my skin.
Someone said, "Red to yellow are your true colors."
Primary colors   Wear them primarily painted
on your face,   not on creased sleeves or woven into

bloodless lace   Wear the paint on your face
and you will hear the flocked flight of primal wings.

A deep tint rises to the surface.
It sings to the ends of my being.
It rides on the span of my skin,
as I want to rise and be more
to be more of an
Indian.

Grandma Friend   rocks within herself   white hair
deep skin   Her hands are a linking fan of prayer.
A braid is buried in her dresser drawer
laid up against the faded pictures
like she said, "Someone took a squaw, that's all,
it's been two hundred years and by now
who cares if my hair is full of feathers?"

I once had another grandmother,
with glinting copper hair
minted in 1907.
She said,
that she didn't like sallow skin
even if it was tanned,
and that she didn't care at all for yellow,
and that she didn't care who she hurt,
(If it's the truth. . . . .
                              It's the truth.)
I brushed the lint from my yellow skirt
and pinched some pinkness in my cheeks,
(What she meant was, she didn't want grandkids
looking too much like Indians.)
The truth was

Grandmothers should have silver hair like Indian nickels.
Aunt Ollie said,
that people, "Were as tall as an Indian,"
and she sang,
"One little, two little, three little
Indians,"
She should know   she was five feet ten
and she said, "That was tall for my time."
In the summer sun   when she hoed
in her garden   in rows
she became lean and brown and native
but, still she wore a flowered apron
and had pale, pale eyes.
On the sprout of spring,
on shaded days beginning before dawn,
she would say, brushing the black earth
from her palms,
"Certain seeds won't wait for the sun."

Sometimes I move swiftly and silently through leaves
breathing in the earth's sweetness with such need
such need as I feel the start, the moving of someone with me.
The birds make no sound as I move.
And no one knows that at night when the moon is deep
and dark and far away—
I squat down as the drum in my heart,
the drum in my heart continues to beat,
and on the ground, the silent ground
                    I count my many
                    beads.

— *Susan Sheppard*

CONVALESCENCE

When you were sick
when you were raped in prison
injured in the war and afraid
sickened by bodies on the ground
and laughter rising from the boots
that kicked them, when you wanted
to spend the night with me talking
constantly talking, the lights blaring—

I nursed, stayed with you, believed
as you grew strong you would be gentle,
would see softly, like someone whose eyes
are held by delicate stems that feel
the shudder and pain of others.

But, now that you can sleep again
and work and go out alone at night,
when you come home you are restless.
I find you pacing your room, hacking
always hacking at the flowers
I placed there, the curtains.
The frightening creatures
that once filled your sleep
now try to invade mine.

Your eyes break off from their roots.
They come out wild at me.

— *Betsy Sholl*

THE FLOOD

Hiding from dust
records of our lives
lie face down under the bed.
Certificates, diplomas, photographs,
love letters from a time
your thighs were so finely tuned
they rippled when my breath passed over.

Yet we never left our bodies.
Our flesh stayed in its banks.
We never expected to wake one morning
water swirling among trees,
water on the front step
slipping under the door.

*

The river breaks through the house.
A trumpet. Our documents are raised.
They are all found lacking.
They stick to the walls, ink
running down in streaks.

*

Tonight, everything lost
wanting rises, bursts
into fullness. Don't move, love.
Don't even speak my name.

Wind we have known
only in passing
tonight kindles our hair.

Tonight, tonight
whatever we let go
returns once with wings
a sprig in its mouth
then leaves.

*

We come back with rakes
gloves, shots against typhoid.

The river makes small confused rills
around an oiltank, sofa, stove
it doesn't remember taking.

We throw out, we burn
mattresses, insulation, books,
photographs of my dead father
his face bloated, covered with silt.

Silt rises through floorboards
each time we scrub. Smoke
drifts through blossoming trees.

My love
this flesh is rising.
It is level with your eyes.
It pours through my fingers.
Our lives are swirling away.

— *Betsy Sholl*

CLEARING THE WAY

Hands grip and slide
against the hickory handle,
muscles remembering unused paths,
as tender hands
return to the axe.
The narrow tree
spits chips,
accepting the steel
with a final spasm:
shower of redbud blossoms.

— *Larry Simpson*

LANDMARK

Last winter,
here was a house
where the poor lived:

weather was everywhere —
under the blankets,
under the plates and cups;
under the stack of firewood
after the last tree was cut
out of the yard; under the table
dismembered for kindling,
and under the chair — snow

settled everywhere
on the porch
as it was dismantled, and room by room
until the stove stood alone

and, taking nothing with them,
the family moved on.

— *Bennie Lee Sinclair*

MY GRANDMOTHER

After the stroke,
I expected her to lift up
on milken wings, out the bright window and up
to her dream place, but she only lay

trying to pick print roses
off of the sheet
to give me, years coming loose instead
in the name she spoke,

whenever I leaned close,
of my dead brother. He sat on the bed with us
while she entertained, performing
her intricate string tricks

without string . . . Jacob's Ladder, Everlasting . . .
myself remembering
what truth her hands used to weave,
for us. Before we drifted or died

we were safe on her drying sheets,
among apples, surveying a world she raked clean
while the strange tall shapes of her fire
parted over us, into disuse —

but while others only acquired
she treated her wounds with salve
made out of herself, applied
each time she caught us

dancing among her projects: little seedlings.
Eventually, she took to embroidering air
so violently
the doctors ordered her tied

and I felt, of my own time, deceived
she should not brighten and lift
out of those restraints. Her plenty,
soaked and peeled and stored

beneath the house-floor,
rots, but roses she did not grow
I hold,
a gift of her infinite weaving.

— *Bennie Lee Sinclair*

LINES

Anchoring, I watched him climb,
His legs still smooth, his ringless hands
Grasping, inching at the cliff,
His eyes turned upward toward my own,
My own down-smiling at my son,
Trying not to look beyond
At what lay a thousand feet below
We climbed, he climbed, his hair blown wild,
His fear clenched tight between his teeth,
Our courage on raw fingertips.

And then a piton went. He fell
Into the space that welcomed him
And toward the rocks that waited. . . .
My hand, not knowing, reached far out,
Reached empty into empty air.
The mountain turned him upside down,
And then the falling stopped.

He dangled there—

A diver diving half a sky,
His body limp,
Suspended on a nylon line
Drawn taut, mere twisting from his waist
To mine, from which that life,
Now saved, now caught,
Now breathing far beyond my own,
Had come.

— *Barbara Smith*

CENTURY #1, PORTRAIT OF A COALTOWN

It is there,
One house the still brown of company property,
Another new with aluminum siding,
One man old and permanently gray like his shovel,
Another young on the longwall.
And the tipple sighs,
Good at least for processing
Somebody else's mine,
Good enough at least
For a coat of blue paint.
And in the cab of the dusty pick-up
He tells of the days
When the baseball diamond
Now in the velveting sunset
Lay virile and sang
Under a triple by Zara
And a Zirkle homerun.
The baselines grow long
With everlasting grass,
The backstop rusty through the weeds.
He brings an echo from the coal-hard hills
Of the Century that is still there.

— *Barbara Smith*

THE LUMINOSITY OF LIFE
after Doris Ullman

All the mothers and fathers here in sickness,
in health, in Ullman's black-and-whites
pretend not to be dying. *Where are they?*

Look close at the head against the hickory,
that man who lies at the picnic's end
by his wife on their best bedsheet,
their eyes feigning sleep, closed.

When did that happen? Who are they?
They are about to wake up and father you.

What about the river they crossed? The same,
hardening somewhere, become a new road.

A certain light evokes itself, some distress
they never escape—you can't deny this.
Yes, it plays like the distant chords of banjos
tickling in a sleeper's dream

                          and, as Ullman saw,
endless, begun. Light on those child-mothers,
the roccoco coils of the weather-withered
boardinghouse in Tuscaloosa.
                          But who
speaks for that man about to crumple
backward when the chair legs break, the sun topples?
The fat woman, naked in the top corner window.

West Virginia **Book Festival**

Abbreviated Schedule

Upstairs Conference Rooms
Friday: 11:00-12:00 Storytelling;
1:00-3:00, Young Writers Workshops;
2:30-4:30 Book Discussion, Poetry Workshop.
Saturday: 11:00-12:30, Losing Geography Panel;
2:30-3:30, Sharyn McCrumb.

Program Map

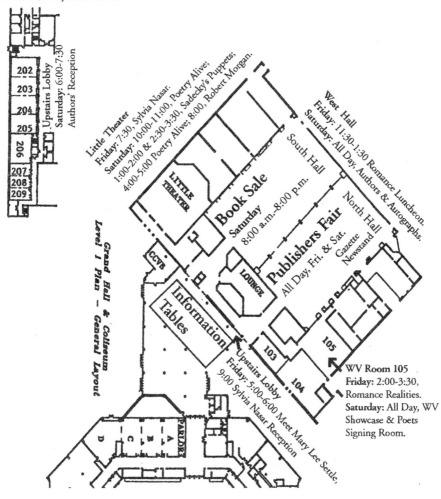

WV Room 105
Friday: 2:00-3:30,
Romance Realities.
Saturday: All Day, WV
Showcase & Poets
Signing Room.

Parlors A,B,C,D
Friday: 1:00-2:00, Gardening (Zeb Wright), Victor Thacker, John O'Brien;
2:30-4:00, Cooking (Rosalie Gaziano), John Cuthbert.
Saturday: 9:30-10:30, Getting Published Panel, Book Collecting (Gordon Simmons), Ancella Bickley,
Sylvia Nasar; 1:00-2:00, Multicultural Literature (Phyllis Moore), Read Aloud (Jody Cottrill), Richard
Currey, Gail Adams; 4:00-5:00, Mystery Panel, History Panel, Stephen Coonts, Gerald Milnes.

Schedule for Friday, October 12

11:00 — 12:00
Storytelling: Marc Harshman and Cheryl Ryan   (Conf. Rm. 202)

11:30 — 1:30
Romance Lovers Luncheon (West Hall)

1:00 — 2:00
(1) *Gardening by the Book* (Parlor A) Zeb Wright

(2) *French Harding: Confederate From West Virginia* (Parlor B) Victor Thacker

(3) *At Home in the Heart of Appalachia* (Parlor D) John O'Brien

1:00 — 3:00
Workshops for Young Writers (Grades 9-12): (Conf. Rm. 207) Marc Harshman
                                                                    (Conf. Rm.208) Cheryl Ryan

2:00 — 3:30
Romance Realities (Rm. 105) Dianne Castell, Lori Foster, Rosemary Laurey

2:30 — 3:30
(1) *Through the Seasons: Making Cooking Easy, Joyful, and Healthy*
                                                            (Parlor A) Rosalie Gaziano
2:30 — 4:00
(2) *Early Art and Artists in West Virginia: Rediscovering a Fine Arts Tradition*
                                                            (Parlor B) John Cuthbert
2:30 — 4:30
(3) *Poetry Writing Workshop for Adults* (Conf. Rm. 203) Maggie Anderson

(4) *Book Discussion of Gap Creek*   (Conf. Rm. 204-205) Robert Morgan

5:00 — 6:00   *Meet Mary Lee Settle* (Upstairs Lobby)

7:30 — 9:00
McCreight Lecture in the Humanities:"A Beautiful Mind" (Little Theater)
         Sylvia Nasar   *Sponsored by the West Virginia Humanities Council*
Reception Following (Upstairs Lobby)
                    Both events are free and open to the public

All Day Activities   Publishers Fair, Bookmobile, Make-it/Take-it Crafts,
Gazette Newsstand & Read-to-Me Corner, Kanawha County Schools
Literature Fair

Schedule for Saturday, October 13

9:30 -- 10:30

(1) *Getting Published* (Parlor A) Pinckney Benedict. Martin Clark,
Meredith Willis

(2) *Introduction to Book Collecting* (Parlor B) Gordon Simmons

(3) *The Life of Memphis Tennessee Garrison and the Use of Oral History*
(Parlor C) Ancella Bickley

(4) *Writing Biography: Learning From Others' Lives* (Parlor D) Sylvia Nasar

---

10:00 — 11:00 *Poetry Alive!* (Little Theater)

11:00 -- 12:30
Panel—Losing Geography: Finding Self (Conf. Rms. 202-205)
Robert Morgan, Denise Giardina, Carlene Thompson

11:15 *(Line up for Storybook Parade)* (North Hall)
11:30 — 12:30 *Gazette Storybook Character Parade* (North Hall)

1:00 -- 2:00

(1) *From Every Mountainside: The Multicultural Literature of West Virginia*
(Parlor A) Phyllis Moore

(2) *Read Aloud Training* (Parlor B) Jody Dodd Cottrill

(3) *The Writing Life* (Parlor C) Richard Currey

(4) *Invention of Character* (Parlor D) Gail Adams

(5) *Sadeckys Puppets* (Little Theater)

1:00 — 3:00 *Workshops for Young Writers (Grades 6-8)*
(1) Marc Harshman (Conf. Rm. 206)   (3) Cheryl Ware (Conf. Rm. 208)
(2) Cheryl Ryan (Conf. Rm. 207)   (4) Anna Smucker (Conf. Rm. 209)

All Day Activities   Book Sale, Authors & Autographs Room, WV Authors
Showcase, Publishers Fair, Bookmobile, Make-it/Take-it Crafts, *Gazette*
Newsstand & Read-to-Me Corner, Kanawha County Schools Literature Fair

Schedule for Saturday, October 13 (Continued)

2:30 -- 3:30

(1) *Sharyn McCrumb "Musical Echoes in Fiction"* (Rms. 202-205)

(2) *Sadeckys Puppets* (Little Theater)

4:00 -- 5:00

(1) *Writing Mystery: Clues to the Genre* (Parlor A) William Hoffman,
John Billheimer, Carlene Thompson

(2) *Bringing History to the Public* (Parlor B) John Williams,
Lon Savage, Ken Hechler

(3) *Writing Fiction: Lies For Fun and Profit* (Parlor C) Stephen Coonts

(4) *WV Folk Culture* (Parlor D) Gerald Milnes

(5) *Poetry Alive!* (Little Theater)

6:00 – 7:30

Authors' Reception (Ticketed Admission Only—Upstairs Lobby)

8:00 – 9:30

Robert Morgan : "The Voice of the Story" (Little Theater)

All Day Activities   Book Sale, Authors & Autographs Room, WV Authors Showcase, Publishers Fair, Bookmobile, Make-it/Take-it Crafts, *Gazette* Newsstand & Read-to-Me Corner, Kanawha County Schools Literature Fair

---

For complete information and descriptions of
the programs and activities on this schedule,
check the 12-page tabloid insert in
The Sunday Gazette Mail for October 7, 2001
(available at the information table)

The silk in her lap, lustrous somehow *(Please?),*
somehow knows, doesn't give a damn for tomorrow,
which pretends it isn't ever coming back.

Every face in this land knows what a lie is.

— *Dave Smith*

POEM FOR AUNT REBECCA

here I'll make an Adam here an Eve
how ready then she was I remember
to breathe her breath into creation
building up a little boy's dreams that way
the finest old fashioned woman imaginable
touching the live white primal dough
yes once she existed realer than I

yes and her dresske rose yivvering
though ironed to white cokeynut perfection
as she hurried down Mill Creek Road
twas the whole goosepimple range
which arrove piff puff
in pokeydot love pox
spip spap speckled to a T
HE WAS MY BEAU
and the midnight cloudburst falling
at her wet inventive lightning face

like a goddam bull I tell you

— *Bob Snyder*

NO REGRETS

Your good looks
were the brownest words in the almanac
the fifth largest planet
the new element and the world series:

your face was naive
like a chronicle caught in a lie
a fox in a garden
not knowing how good looking how naive how naive;

I was an animal out of a book
and you were pure progress
but steps had been taken
assumptions had been made:

you hurried me off
when we quit seeing one another
sweeping the sidewalk the cut grass
sorry saying sorry sweeping sorry goodbye

— *Bob Snyder*

THE SQUARE DANCE

Inside the house three men, one old and two just boys
Are talking with their fiddles, asking
"Let's see can we get us aholt of a tune?"

Dogs are running with us kids.
Where do they all come from in the night?
With their yips and yowls and the fiddles complaining and
Our halloos and the grinding of the gears of the Ford
Cars and the bats skipping on the waves of air
We toss over our whirling heads
The night is getting better every minute.

I stand off and watch the kids and dogs.
You can hear them in the big shadows
Then they hit the eye like a lantern slide when they
Come into the window light.
Its like the house-inside is coming out to grab us,
To finger us out of the dark, and it will
In a little while.

I'm twelve and in a new dress.
Everybody looks at me at one time or another,
Not all at once because I don't shine yet
But they look like I remind them of something good like
Catching a fish or going to the Fair,
And they say easy things to me
To keep me growing up.
There's a blooming jasmine in the Mackendree's yard
That drives me wild with its longing sweetness.
The wind tries to unburden it and carry off its smell
But it keeps as much as it gives away.

"Here's a flower for you, you ugly thing."
That's James handing me one of the heavy, witching blossoms.
He means I'm pretty but he wants to not like me
As much as he does.

We see everybody's gone inside but us
So like two lagging fish in a school
We let the retreating currents of their grown-up talk
And grown-up way of walking slowly up the steps
Onto the porch and through the door
Pull us in.
There's only some young men outside now
Drinking cider.

Pretty soon one of them comes in
And asks me for the first dance.
I get funny-feeling and quiet but he kids me out of it
And I start to think maybe I'm suddenly a whole lot older.
Here we go, "do si do."
I see flashes of faces go by, all smiling
Except James who is laughing to show he doesn't care.

Dancing round and round
My heart spins up to the ceiling.
I feel like a seed pod in a whirlwind
With a big bowl of sunlight showering its sparkles over me
To the tune of "Bird in the Cage," then I see
Its just the kerosene lamps flickering on their stands
Each time the fiddlers stomp the floor.
I sure do dance good tonight.
Bradshaw, my new grown-up boyfriend is telling me
He's scared of my Pa
Or he'd come take me out. I wouldn't want to go out
With him, but now that he's scared to ask me,

I'm having a lot more fun being a woman.
I'm wearing heels, by the way,
And a very tight belt to make it look
Like I've got a figger, Oh, Lord!
How I love to flirt.

I'm not the only one.
Old Mrs. Zeigler with her poor clothes
And her hungry, black eyes
Is dancing with a fat, young preacher.
They forget anybody else is here,
They like each other so well. He wobbles his hauch
Up by her flat old hip to promenade
And wobbles off again, looking kind and happy.
She looks as wild as a caught raccoon. No man
Has liked her in years and her good luck makes her crazy,
A little bit. She's tossing that motheaten shawl
Like she's asking a bull to charge her head-on.
You have to notice her big calves and skinny ankles
Because she lifts her skirt
And stomps the floor like she's killing snakes
With her sharp hooves.

The preacher wobbles around her
Watching the show with a boy's glad face.
All I can say is, "I hope I never."

Now its time for refreshments.
I'm sitting with James who acts like he might move away
Because I'm so grown-up I scare him,
But he stays and we eat cake.

I know I'm going to dream all night about Bradshaw.
I'm going to dream of how it will be in a few years

When we go out and sit in his car
And he can kiss me.
My feet will drop off, for sure.

James hasn't got sense enough to walk me home
So I go home with my brother, the way I came,
Him carrying his fiddle and me
Carrying my high heeled shoes.

— *Charlotte St. John*

MRS. HENRITZE

Mrs. John Buford Henritze
was twice president
of the Woman's Missionary Society
(whose members met in circles
for programs with prayers,
desserts and non-alcoholic beverages,
their collections going to support
the work of missionaries
in such ungodly places
as India and the Belgian Congo)
of the Buford Memorial
Methodist Episcopal Church, South.

On the first Sunday of each month
Mrs. Henritze attired like Solomon
would progress down the aisle
to the altar for Holy Communion,
would kneel on a tufted velvet-covered cushion
for a cube of dry bread and Welch's Grape Juice.

A small, unheated building
isolated and seldom entered
sees Mrs. Henritze
suffer slow combustion,
in a sealed berth of stone
containing a copper coffin
containing a mahogany coffin
that robbers one day will open
to wrest from the skeleton
the gold, the pearls, and the diamonds
with which she planned to astonish the angels
upon her arrival in heaven.

— *Paul Curry Steele*

COAL

Black gold of Appalachia,
hill-patterned pillage,
yours is the curse of the conquered.
You, who could have summoned
laughter from a mountain sky,
your augered veins lie tracked
to golden coastal cities;
and as conquistadores cabal
there, you, condemned,
cry blackness over the land.

— *Jim Stokely*

THIS LAND, FULL OF SAID REGIONS

full of coal roads slanting from the highways,
winding to those hells hidden not from the sky,
pitting the mountains,
turning the creeks to clay
turning the farms to clay;
this land full of housing by the rivers,
no homes but in the flood plain,
old miners, lost,
resting on lawn chairs lapped by lespedeza;
this land that could have been and was busted down,
home of something never here
a snake coiling fire from the wet easy earth—
for this land nothing waits save death and time
and the cows which look up from their stirrings,
astonished, four-square, brazen.

— *Jim Stokely*

MARTHY

I know why they kept you poor and cast
you with the children and the dafter servants:
you were beautiful a fact recorded
in the dusty fall of 1897.
Caroline and Nannie
each married the same man
passed the pride of bearing sons
from one to the other. Omitting you.
A changling. No pie-faced Scottish lass surely.
Surely the sheened and tapered daughter
of a rich Polish Jew.

150

Through a Great War and a Great Depression
your mournful letters beckoned the brother/cousins
home to Christmas and Easter.
Finally there was only you.
In your dresses long as trousers
eyes like blackened silver.
You wound your lustrous hair to strings
planted on the light of the moon
what should have gone to ground on the dark.
The brother/cousins slipped the shrinking matrix.
The suburbs cropped the land.
They say I stir a pot like you
my knees and ankles inept in company
my arms too flimsy fingers too flexuous
for the pitcher. But I am not beautiful
not alien enough in my looks
to have dusted the decent mantles til they cracked
do not have the fearful purpose
to wear deserted porches like a shawl
grace a staircase's uncoiling.
What you must have seen in your flights
past the dusty mirrors of that barren place.
Undone. Gone to ground both.
The house pulled down made parking
for the reservoir.
The boys they recalled
your maelstrom eyes your taut mouth over the boiling pot
grin and glitter under the man's hat
leaning lamplight the hiss
you could have been their mother.
They laid you with Caroline and Nannie
in the square with the tallest obelisk.

— *Nancy Stone*

151

NEXT DOOR

I have never seen the sun shine
or heard a soft wind blow
children's laughter to the tree tops
for no other children go
to that house, that lonely white house
with no curtain at the door
and no smells of supper cooking
drifting through the darkness. More
and more I come to stop and listen,
look and wonder what life gives
of its warmth, richness, and happiness
to the house where Sophie lives.

— *Jane Stuart*

LOVE CHILD

Your mouth is full of flower words,
blue roses hinged upon thin stems
of grass.
You spit them out, and squeeze
dry tears
to slide across my toes
and sizzle on a sunny scone of rock.
I bite your lips,
and kiss your eyes,
but you
can not be startled from this mumbling sleep,
the core of your green apple hours.

— *Jane Stuart*

GRANDFATHER AT THE WINDOW

I cannot say where he is,
my grandfather milking by braille
before dawn. He took me in
and held me when I would not kill
squirrels with my father's rifle.

Darkness gathered the family
for supper. He was late
digging out the back pasture
for skulls, beads, other indian letters.
Rocks in his head, grandma'd cry
cut more carrots for the stew.

I cannot say how he knew
the indians cared. Why it seemed
the neighbors were always bankers,
or hunters, landless farmers, welfare
cheats, who'd finally lost the words.

He was foolish, coughing and digging
when he was sick, so delighted
at a piece of sculptured turtle
his beard'd be suddenly so long
it soaked up the water table,
tangled in the apple orchard roots.

Old men might die of neglect
whittling on country store stoops.
Younger men with their rolled sleeves
and brown masks might deny
I could love them. And grandfather

would weep, hold my hands to the moon
in his window before he could vanish
and I could sleep.

— *Steve Rasnic Tem*

A WOMAN
(Who Could Be Appalachian)

There were mountains
around the town where
                          she grew up

and down the narrow
valley ran one set of tracks
                          and down these tracks
came one train

every two days

She balanced on the rails
barefoot   all the way
to the deepest hole
where she swam naked
                          with crawdads and snakes

Her aunt   who became
an alcoholic
after her husband left
with another woman
taught her to cast
                          without tangling
and gave her hand-me-downs

Her best friend Martha
  who was poor
lived on a farm
                and it was there
she learned to quilt
milk and churn and
                where pigs really come from

On Saturdays   in the old
pickup   she came
to town with Martha
and her people   blending
into the crowded stores

empty on other days

and pretending
she did not live
                two blocks from Main Street

She belonged to 4-H
F.H.A. and M.Y.F.—mainly
for the hayrides—and
                lost her virginity

in the back seat
of her high school sweet-
heart's secondhand car
parked out the dirt road
                behind old Annie Overholt's
chicken farm

On Career
Day she had no

answer
Pressed   she guessed
she would marry
and even today
although he jilted her
                    she still feels guilty

She is also guilty
for the lines
in her mother's still-
young face
her father's stoic
sweat   and the awful
nameless crime of
                    being alive

To escape shame
she went on to college
even finished   but still
                    is wary of cemetaries
sidewalk cracks   black
cats   and swears
                    the moon
controls her moods

The Wrath of God
will always override
                    Sartre

On certain summer days
passing damp
concrete alleys
she gets a smell of
                    her grandmother's cellar

where her cousins always
found her   hiding
when she screamed at
                    popping jars

Now she stops
at farmer's market
loads up   spends
hours working

for that same opaque gleam
                        that same perfect seal

Meeting her austere
expression at a bluegrass
festival   you would think
her a snob
                    not knowing

her fear of strangers

She saves plastic
containers   paper bags
rubber bands and scraps
of cloth she stitches
together on winter evenings
after lesson plans

                        She would die

if her friends knew
about her hope chest

— *Julia Thomas*

ENCOUNTER

The big stones of the chimney behind the house
soaked up my grandmother
her face is smooth, young again
within the polished stone
she used to whet her blades.
Her hair is no longer gray.

I crawl in and out of the mortar
like an insect under a door
recall my youth
my grandmother's face wrinkles again
her hair turns gray
I can not stay

I take my knife
whet the wrinkles smooth with rapid strokes
across the polished stone.

— *Rudy Thomas*

THREATENING CONDITIONS

jet passing in the night

wind brisk from the southwest

words spaced upon the page

like seeds in a row

far-off thunder

more words

beware

a poem.

— *Rudy Thomas*

THE DAY THE X-MAN CAME

I lived in my house
   for 33 years
Before the flood came,
   before the land let loose its
                tears.
I thought that if you worked
   hard 33 years, well
Then just 12 more
    and you could sit and rest
              a spell.

Why,
    I remember one corner of
            the house
        was leanen and fallen in
        33 years ago.
            When my old man came
                    haulen in
            wood and blocks and we
                    set in
To builden year by year,
            builden what we never had
                    before.
It was slow, hard to see
        any end to the builden
            and hammeren,
                    but
We saved that corner, built
            it back-
laid away and saved and
            raised five more
        to lay away and save.

All our lives
We ain't never missed a day
    of payen some way,
Doing the best we can,
        But I'm 53 and
        He's 62
        And it's way too late for them
            E-Z credit plans

            Carpet, couch, the family
                    tree,
            Baby shoes and Bible too
            Went floaten on down to

Kermit and Crum
Floaten away to Kingdom
Come.
And I know they
Ain't no amount of misery
Gonna bring them sweet
things
Back to me
And I know it, I know it, I
know it

But I still can't see
Why we gotta pay
Them Judas strippers to
haul us away.

How on earth can we
stand
Selling our land
On the installment plan?
And all them politicians that
never do
nothing but pat me on the
back
and tell a lie or two.
Later or sooner, it's all
overdue
them flood's garnisheed
me
they'll garnishee you.

Well, it took all of them years,
All 33,
Floods and floods and barrels
of tears

To bring me to this day
And I sit and I cry and I wail
                        and I moan.
But no amount of hurt and
                        pain's
        Gonna float me back my
                        home.

So I just sit and wait
    for the X-Man to come
            burn my builden down

                Not much else to say
                33 years
                washed away

— *Jim Webb*

HOPE BOX

The box, veneer, is from the thirties.
Your husband shows the treasures you laid back—
I rub my finger on your nightgown. Peachglow
Pale silk. Three roses hand-embroidered
At the neck. Given by the girls at the mill
Before your marriage. It lies folded
Tissue wrapped.
Below, I find your bedspreads. One—
Heavy white chenille. Off a line in Georgia
From your trip to Disney World.
Twenty-five dollars even then.
Another's from the neighbors
Before your move to town. Magenta threaded geometrics.
In a basket (used each Easter
for the children) your pictures wait:
A now forgotten girl
Posing in a strapless prom dress. One of you
That day you caught the biggest croaker
On the York. And here,
With you, your Sears and Roebuck suited suitor
Hair slicked, waiting for your father's blessing.
You smile
Holding your new suede purse.
Frayed, it keeps your pennies here—all Indian heads
The last savages. Saved back.
For tomorrow
For a pine box
For us who live among your hoard.

— *Beth Wellington*

BEA HENSLEY HAMMERS AN IRON CHINQUAPIN LEAF ON HIS ANVIL NEAR SPRUCE PINE AND COGITATES ON THE NATURE OF TWO BEAUTY SPOTS

in the Linville Gorge I
know this place

now it's a rock wall
you look up
it's covered in punktatum all
the way to Heaven

that's a sight

**

up on Smoky
you ease up at daybust
and see the first
light in the tops of the tulip trees

now boys that just naturally
grinds and polishes
the soul

makes it
normal
again

I mean it's really
pretty!

— *Jonathan Williams*

THE HERMIT CACKLEBERRY
BROWN ON HUMAN VANITY:

caint call your name
but your face is easy

come sit

now some folks figure theyre
bettern
cowflop they
aint

not a bit

just good to hold the world together
like hooved up ground

thats what

— *Jonathan Williams*

RUINS

in my great-grandfather's house
are many memories
it is so and I am telling you
of those memories
of my last pilgrimage to
that eroding time capsule
perched desolate
on an outgrowth hill
moated by a lifeless stream

the day was fair
the sky bright
a new road splayed out
of the earth carrying
a caravan of coal trucks
for the strip mines
the dirt was still raw
but blackberries were red
raspberries ripening
I picked daisies
laurel
azalea
pale pink wild roses
and put the blossoms
in my hair

the sun was hot
but the trees were tall
virgin timber shading
the way to the ruins
my grandfather you see
allowed no one to live there

the forty years since
the old man died
I once played by
the empty house
in the scented plum orchard
used the swing Grandad
built for Ona the child
of his second marriage
(7 at the time of my birth)
and when I launched out
toes touching branches
the world lay miles below
the swing is now absent
from the pear tree before
the once-handsome frame

two-storied
it was always painted gray
and happier days had seen
a roof of wooden shingles
now boards are sprung apart
its tin roof dissolving in rust
the pepper vine
my great-grandmother planted
(she was a Renfrew)

is a monster parasite
threading through
its vines thick as an arm
bulging over and under
timbers and windowframes
she also put down a cedar
in the yard and always said
that when it grew high enough

to shade her grave
she would die
only a lightning-struck stump
still stands five feet high

the side door swung wide
and inside a dusky suit and
yellowed shirt hung loosely
on the wall
vandals came calling
but did not touch those
clothes at all fearing
perhaps the ghost of the
rambunctious doctor
the mantelpiece
and fireplace stones
wrenched violently free
silently still an ancient
rumor of hidden cash

catalog and newspaper pages
used for insulation
swag from the ceiling like
clumps of powdery Spanish moss
broad and once well-scrubbed
floorboards sway back
half the stairs have fallen in
dockweed shot up like rockets
through the yard
ridges of rusty tin flop
from the eaves

a haphazard timpanist
when the wind stirs
a short-horned heifer
resented my being there
I looked at the sluggish creek
the rust of acid run-off
staining the earth
like dried blood
cradled my head
against the pear tree
and cried quietly
and for a long time

later I stopped again
at Grandad's place
took fading flowers from
my hair and wreathed them
round the cedar stump

— *Shirley Williams*

COMMENTS ON AN AMERICAN VISIT IN VIETNAM
(inspired by Michael Casey)

1. *message*

anderson lifted
            the flap of his tent to
        take a leak last night
    it was dark
i couldn't see his face but i
        could still see the way he looked clearing
        bodies off the landing zone that
                                afternoon
and i got the message

    it was in his open weeping:
        he just didn't give a damn anymore
    which flag he was pissin' on

2. *something lost in the translation*

jr   that is   the kid came
never goes   not since the   running out of
anywhere   night he   the jungle
without his   chopped that   screaming
dictionaries anymore   little boy   HOA BINH, Hoa Ky
                       in two with   HOA BINH
                       his M-sixteen   jr keeps translating
                                         it to himself
                                         PEACE, UNITED STATES
                                         PEACE

jr never goes anywhere without his dictionaries anymore

170

3. *traveling companions*

in school
they always said that
hitler was evil
for burning the
jews
and
bombing england
i saw him the other night
i was about to slit his throat
when nixon got on the train
with a suitcase full of napalm
under his arm
"hello, adolph, how's business?"
after the porter told me
they always traveled together
i jumped off the train near atlantis
and got stoned
on old campaign buttons and
                    nazi armbands
is school out yet?

— *Marty Wilson*

SENTENCES

The ash fish has been away for a long time now,
The snow transparent; a white cane rakes back and forth
In the hush, no sweet sound from the leaves.

Whatever is dead stays dead: the lighted and cold
Blue blank pavilions of the sky,
The sand, the crystal's ring in the bushy ear—
Voices logy with sleep, their knapsacks
The color of nothing, full of the great spaces they still must
cross.

The trees take care of their own salvation, and rocks
Swell with their business; and there, on the clean cloth
Of the river, a Host is floating without end.

Heaven, that stray dog, eats on the run and keeps moving.

— *Charles Wright*

JANUARY

In some other life
I'll stand where I'm standing now, and will look down,
                                        and will see
My own face, and not know what I'm looking at.

These are the nights
When the oyster begins her pearl, when the spider slips
Through his wired rooms, and the barns cough, and the
                                        grass quails.

— *Charles Wright*

REQUIEM

He loaded the shot gun
as absently as he lighted his cigarette,
remembering NaTrang and rice paddies,
wrinkling his nose as he recalled
the stink of the Far East.

He had been grateful to come home whole,
stepping from the American 727 at Cleveland
Hopkins with a bronze star in his pocket;
shrapnel dark blue in his left leg.

The war remained a time-bomb in his duffle,
dioxin masquarading as other ailments:
the blisters wouldn't heal, headache baked his
vision, but he was able to stand despite numbness.
Anger sank like stones in his belly.

He lay sky-shrunk against a gravel parking lot,
pupils pinpoints of questions, a pink
froth bubbled at the corner of his mouth:

the life a bullet
making a small mark at entry
taking so much when it leaves.

— *Barbara Yount*

IN A QUIET LARDER

In a quiet larder
thoughts of murder
are measured out.
In an open field
someone says he's
not his sister's keeper.

I see by your shape
you're as clouded
thin hungry as the rest
of them. I lean
against the door say no
no you can't come in
weak as any who never
went for power and that
after all is most of us.

— *Isabel Zuber*

FROM THE GARLIC PATCH

If it rains long enough
the leak will drill through
roof and ceiling
spread a puddle
on the floor. I used
to worry about such things—
now I leave them alone.
Someone else can battle rust,
mold and what creeps up to the door.
I haven't sewn on a button
in ages and smoke from the fire
gives me a cough. It's no longer
important to be neat—certainly
not to be clean or clever.
Let bygones be drybones. I'll
stew what I've got, eat it
when I want to.
Why don't you go wear down
your broom on your own porch?
One of these nights
I'll ride naked over all of you.

— *Isabel Zuber*

ABOUT THE POETS
c. 1980

RAY ALLEN, a teacher and filmmaker, has worked and studied in Kentucky and Califormia. "Sorghum Harvest" is one of a series of poems about returning to the land. He now lives in Virginia.

GAIL AMBURGEY, born and raised on Buffalo Creek in West Virginia, was one of the founders of the Soupbean Poets of Antioch/Appalachia. Her poems have appeared in *What's A Nice Hillbilly Like You...*, *Mucked*, and *New Ground*.

MAGGIE ANDERSON, a West Virginia native, has worked extensively as a poet-in-the-schools, prisons, mental hospitals, and nursing homes. Her collection, *Years That Answer*, was published by Harper & Row in 1980, and she has recently completed a book of essays on poetry and community called *Hunting with the Heart*.

BOB HENRY BABER lives in Charleston, West Virginia, and teaches at the Southern Appalachian Labor School. He lists the invention of the Lowku form as one of his greatest literary achievements.

COLEMAN BARKS, born in Chattanooga, Tennessee, teaches English at the University of Georgia. His book, *The Juice*, was published by Harper in 1971. He has also published two chapbooks, *New Words* and *We're Laughing at the Damage*.

JOSEPH BARRETT was born in Montgomery, West Virginia, and now lives in Lexington, Kentucky. His first chapbook was *Periods of Lucidity*.

JOE BASILONE lives in Belington, West Virginia. This poem is from a collection entitled *Interstate Afternoon*.

CARLEY REES BOGARD, born and educated in West Virginia, currently teaches at the State University of New York, New Paltz. "My Father's Black Lungs" first appeared in *A Magazine of Appalachian Women*.

SUSAN BURGESS resides in Charleston, West Virginia, and is a member of West Virginia Writers.

KATHRYN STRIPLING BYER is a widely published poet who has worked as an editor for the *North Carolina Arts Journal*.

JO CARSON lives and works in Johnson City, Tennessee. Besides poetry, she writes short stories and plays.

LILLIE D. CHAFFIN, a Kentucky native, has published children's books (notably *We Be Warm Till Springtime Comes*), as well as collections of poetry, including *A Stone for Sisyphus* and *8th Day, 13th Moon*. She lives in Winchester, Kentucky.

FRED CHAPPELL, novelist and poet, teaches at the University of North Carolina at Greensboro. His collections include *Midquest* and *The World Between the Eyes*.

MARY JOAN COLEMAN was born and raised in the Mt. Nebo area in West Virginia. Her book, *Take One Blood Red Rose*, was published in 1978 by West End Press.

MARK DeFOE, author of *Bringing Home Breakfast*, teaches at West Virginia Wesleyan College, where he edits *Laurel Review*.

VICTOR DEPTA was born in Accoville, West Virginia, and now teaches at the University of Tennessee at Martinsville. His books include *The House* and *The Creek*.

DAVID DOOLEY, formerly of Knoxville, Tennessee, is currently working as a paralegal in Austin, Texas.

GEORGE ELLISON lives with his wife and children in the Smokies near Bryson City, North Carolina. He wrote the biographical introduction to the reissue of Horace Kephart's *Our Southern Highlanders*. These poems are from an on-going gathering entitled *Permanent Camp*.

SYDNEY FARR, who grew up in Red Bird, Kentucky, is a librarian for the Berea College Mountain Collection. Her books include *Appalachian Women: A Bibliography* and *More Than Moonshine*, a cookbook.

JEFFREY FOLKS lives in Athens, Tennessee, where he teaches at Tennessee Wesleyan College.

KITTY FRAZIER teaches at West Virginia State College. A native West Virginian of German-Swiss descent, she is a wife, mother, and champion archer. Her poems have appeared in regional publications.

MARITA GARIN, who received her MFA from Goddard, lives in Johnson City, Tennessee, where she has coordinated the East Tennessee Poetry Series. Her work has been widely published and won her a fellowship from the state Arts Commission.

179

SHARON GINSBURG lives on a farm in central West Virginia, where, in addition to writing, she teaches heritage crafts.

JAMES B. GOODE, a native of Harlan County, Kentucky, now teaches at the University of Kentucky's Southeast Center. His collections include *The Whistle and the Wind* and *Poets of Darkness*.

PAT GRAY has been published in *Poet Lore*, *The Small Farm* and *Calyx*. She lives in Knoxville, Tennessee.

RICHARD HAGUE, a native of Steubenville, Ohio, has published two collections, *Crossings* and *Ripening*. A writer of fiction as well as poetry, he teaches high school in Cincinnati.

PAULETTA HANSEL is from Jackson, Kentucky. She has been a part of Antioch/Appalachia's Soupbean Poets collective and of the Southern Appalachian Writers Coop. She now lives in Cincinnati, Ohio, where she teaches and works with Street Talk, the city's street theatre troupe.

MARC HARSHMAN lives on Bowman Ridge in Marshall County, West Virginia. His chapbook, *Turning Out the Stones*, won the State Street Press competition.

VICKY HAYES, an eastern Kentucky native, works as a journalist in Paintsville. Her work has appeared in *Mountain Review*, and she has published a chapbook, *Night Winds*.

MIKE HENSON lives in Cincinnati, Ohio. His novels include *Ransack* and *A Small Room with Trouble on My Mind*.

IRA HERMAN has returned to Huntington, West Virginia after a stint as managing editor of Mountain State Press. He has one book of poems, *Dark Horses Leaping into Flame.*

SHERRY HOLSTEIN was born and raised on Mason's Creek at Viper in Perry County, Kentucky. She was an early supporter of the Southern Appalachian Writer's Cooperative.

LEE HOWARD, originally from Clay County, Kentucky, works as an industrial sociologist in Tennessee. Her work has appeared in *Southern Exposure, Mother Earth News, Appalachian Journal,* and anthologies such as *Working Culture.* Her book is *The Last Unmined Vein.*

DELORES JACOBS, born and educated in the Southwest, has lived for many years in Knoxville, Tennessee. She has taught English and art and writes fiction as well as poetry.

DAVID JARVIS has been published in *Strokes* and in the *Appalachian Intelligencer.* He currently resides in Huntington, West Virginia, where he works with mental patients.

CAREY JOBE is an attorney who lives in Kingston, Tennessee. His work has been published in *The Plains Poetry Journal* and *The Lyric.*

LOYAL JONES, a North Carolina native, studied at Berea College and the University of North Carolina. A former director of the Council of the Southern Mountains, he now directs the Appalachian Center at Berea College.

RODNEY JONES, originally from Alabama, had published two collections, *Going Ahead Looking Back* and *The Story They Told Us Of Light.* His third book, *The Unborn,* will be out from

Atlantic Monthly Press this spring. Jones now lives in Illinois.

JANE WILSON JOYCE, who grew up in Kingsport, Tennessee, has had poems in *Moving Out, Poet* and *Critic,* and *Adena.* Her chapbook, *The Quilt Poems,* was the first in a series from Mill Springs Press. She teaches at Centre College.

SHEILA JOYCE grew up in eastern Kentucky, graduating from Berea College and the University of Kentucky. She has written songs, feature articles, and several children's plays produced in Louisville, where she has taught English for eighteen years.

GEORGE ELLA LYON, a native of Harlan, Kentucky, was a director of the 1980 Appalachian Poetry Project and one of the editors of this book. Her poems have appeared in *Prairie Schooner, Southern Poetry Review,* and in *Mountain,* a chapbook.

RUSSELL MARANO, originally from West Virginia, studied philosophy at Northwestern University and lived for many years in Illinois. His book is *Poems from a Mountain Ghetto.*

ADRIANNE MARCUS, a native of North Carolina, has published poetry, fiction, and nonfiction. Her poetry collections include *The Moon Is a Marrying Eye, Faced with Love,* and *In Divided Weather* (forthcoming). She works as a free lance writer in San Francisco.

JEFF DANIEL MARION, a Tennessean, works as a farmer, college professor, and editor of Mill Springs Press. His books include *Watering Places; Out in the Country, Back Home;* and *Tight Lines.*

MARGARET McDOWELL, a lifelong resident of Morgantown, West Virginia, has published two books of poetry, *View from College Avenue* and *Our Song, Too.*

MICHAEL McFEE, former editor of *Carolina Quarterly*, has won numerous poetry prizes, and his work has appeared in *American Poetry Review*, *The Nation*, and many other publications. He now lives in Durham, North Carolina.

BONNI McKEOWN, a West Virginia native, has published two books of poetry and prose, *Peaceful Patriot* and *Pieces*. She works as a journalist.

LLEWELLYN McKERNAN lives and teaches in Huntington, West Virginia. Her book, *Short and Simple Annals*, appeared in 1979. Recently she completed a second collection, *Making Herself New*, through a fellowship from the West Virginia Arts and Humanities Commission.

DEVON McNAMARA lives in Phillipi, West Virginia and has been a frequent contributor to *Trellis* and *Grab-a-Nickel.*

LOUISE McNEILL, poet laureate of her native West Virginia, has published *Elderberry Flood*, a state history for children, as well as collections of her poetry, *Gauley Mountain* and *Paradox Hill: From Appalachian to Lunar Shore.*

ALICE McNEW lives in Mt. Sterling, Kentucky, where she teaches piano and serves as the church organist. She has been a participant in the Appalachian Writer's Workshop at Hindman, Kentucky.

EVELYN MILLER grew up in the midwest but has lived in Harlan County, Kentucky, for eleven years. Married and the mother of two daughters, she teaches at the community college.

HEATHER ROSS MILLER, born in the Uwharrie Mountains of North Carolina, has published widely. Her books include *Horse Horse, Tyger Tyger* and *Cofessions of a Champeen Baton Twirler.*

JIM WAYNE MILLER, a native of western North Carolina, attended Berea College and Vanderbilt and now teaches at Western Kentucky University. His principle collections are *Dialogue with a Dead Man, The Mountains Have Come Closer,* and *Vein of Words.*

ELIZABETH MOORE, actress and teacher, was born in Roanoke, Virginia. She has published in a number of literary journals and currently teaches high school in Blount County, Tennessee.

JANICE TOWNLEY MOORE lives in Georgia and teaches at Young Harris College. Her poems have appeared in *Southern Humanities Review, Southern Poetry Review,* and *The Anthology of Magazine Verse.*

MAUREEN MOREHEAD's work has appeared in *Twigs.*

ALLAN MORGAN lives in Knoxville, Tennessee, where he teaches and works as a writer/photographer. His poems have appeared in *Old Hickory Review* and his articles and photographs have been published widely.

ROBERT MORGAN was born in Hendersonville, North Carolina, and grew up on the family farm in neaby Zirconia.

His books include *Zirconia Poems, Red Owl, Groundwork,* and *Bronze Age.* Since 1971 he has taught at Cornell.

DONALD NARKEVIC lives and teaches in Phillipi, West Virginia.

LEE PENNINGTON, playwright, poet, and teacher, has been a force in Appalachian writing for many years. His collections include *Scenes from a Southern Road, I Knew a Woman,* and *April Poems.* He teaches at Jefferson Community College.

RITA QUILLEN has published short stories and criticism as well as poems. She lives on a farm in southwest Virginia and is currently doing a Master's thesis on Appalachian poets.

LARRY RICHMAN teaches composition at Virginia Highlands Community College. He lives near Abingdon with his wife in the house they built out of materials salvaged from the wrecking operation described below.

ANNE RONEY lives in Knoxville, Tennessee, where she is an elementary school supervisor. Her work has appeared in *The Small Farm.*

JOHN RUSSELL, formerly of Fenwick Mountain, West Virginia, where he ran a country store and gas station, now lives in Texas.

TIMOTHY RUSSELL works in a steelmill in Weirton, West Virginia.

BETTIE SELLERS is Chairman of the Humanities Division at Young Harris College in Georgia. Her collections include

Spring Onions and Cornbread, Westward from Bald Mountain, and *Morning of the Red-Tailed Hawk.*

SUSAN SHEPPARD lives in Charleston, West Virginia. Her first collection, *Book of Shadows, Book of Dreams,* was published in 1979. Her work has also appeared in *Rolling Stone* and *Backcountry.*

BETSY SHOLL, originally from New Jersey, lived for seven years in Big Stone Gap, Virginia. Her books are *Changing Faces* and *Appalachian Winter.* She is currently working as a poet-in-the-schools in Maine.

LARRY SIMPSON's work has appeared in *Mountain Review.*

BENNIE LEE SINCLAIR's books include *Little Chicago Suite* and *The Arrowhead Scholar.* She lives with her husband, potter Don Lewis, in a wilderness area in the South Carolina mountains where they have built their home and studios themselves.

BARBARA SMITH is the director of the Humanities Program at Alderson-Broaddus College in Phillipi, West Virginia, where she edits *Grab-a-Nickel.* Her poetry has appeared widely and her novel, *Six Miles Out,* was published by Mountain State Press.

DAVE SMITH, originally from Portsmouth, Virginia, has been a bartender, a teacher, and a high school football coach. His books include *Mean Rufus Thrown Down, A Fisherman's Whore,* and *Cumberland Station,* from which these poems are taken.

BOB SNYDER, formerly the director of Antioch/Appalachian, is now working on his doctorate in Massachusetts. His work has appeared in many places, and his collection is *We'll See Who's a Peasant.*

CHARLOTTE ST. JOHN, who lives in Brevard, North Carolina, has published in *American Heritage* as well as in regional periodicals. She has recently completed a novel.

PAUL CURRY STEELE is originally from Logan, West Virginia, and now lives in Charleston. His work has appeared in *New Ground, Strokes,* and in *Anse on Island Creek and Other Poems,* published by Mountain State Press.

JIM STOKELY grew up in Newport, Tennessee. After college he spent six years as a free-lance writer and then became director of the Children's Museum at Oak Ridge. His collection is *Mummy Truths.*

NANCY STONE was born in Erwin, North Carolina. Her poetry and fiction have appeared in *Sunstone, Worksheet, The Greensboro Review,* and *The Iowa Review.* With Robert Grey she edited *White Trash: An Anthology of Contemporary Southern Poets.*

JANE STUART, originally from Kentucky, now lives in Florida. Her books include *A Year's Harvest, Gideon's Children, Land of the Fox, Yellowhawk,* and *Eyes of the Mole.*

JULIA THOMAS, no biographical material available.

RUDY THOMAS lives and teaches in Albany, Kentucky. His books include *Tornado and Other Poems, The Ground of Memory,* and *War Stories and Other Poems.*

JIM WEBB is a poet, playwright, and swarper. Born in Letcher County, Kentucky, he has been active in publishing and co-edited *Mucked* and *Strokes: Contemporary Appalachian Poetry*. He now lives in Whitesburg, Kentucky, where he edits *Pine Mountain Sand and Gravel*.

BETH WELLINGTON has studied at the Appalachian Writer's Workshop at Hindman, Kentucky. Her work has appeared in *Appalachian Heritage*.

JONATHAN WILLIAMS, a North Carolina poet, has published over seventy-five books, pamphlets, and broadsides, of which the best known are *An Ear in Bartram's Tree, Blues and Roots/Rue and Bluets*, and *Get Hot or Get Out*. In 1951 he founded the Jargon Society, a poet's press for which he serves as editor, publisher, and designer.

SHIRLEY WILLIAMS writes for the Courier-Journal (Louisville, Kentucky) and is a staff member at the Appalachian Writer's Workshop, Hindman, Kentucky.

CHARLES WRIGHT, a native of Pickwick, Tennessee, has published several books of poetry, including *The Dream Animal, Hard Freight,* and *China Trace*. He teaches at the University of California at Irvine.

BARBARA YOUNT has published work in *No Business Poems*.

ISABEL ZUBER catalogues obscure books for the Wake Forest University Library, keeps house for her family, writes and gardens. She grew up in Boone, North Carolina, and is a poetry editor for *The Arts Journal* in Asheville. Her work appeared in *No Business Poems*.

188

ACKNOWLEDGEMENTS

Ray Allen for "Sorgum Harvest" (first appeared in _Appalachian Heritage_, Spring 1979).

Gail Amburgey for "3 A.M. Train" from _We're Alright But We Ain't Special_, © 1976 by Mountain Union Books, Beckley, West Virginia, and "Blood Money" in _Soupbean: An Anthology of Contemporary Appalachian Literature_, © 1977 by Mountain Union Books.

Bob Henry Baber for "Roofing For Aunt Pearl" from _Assorted Life Savers_, © 1976 by Robert Barber, and "Appalachian Spring" (first appeared in _Southern Exposure_, January-February 1982).

Joe Barrett for "Fainting Angels" (first appeared in _Pig Iron_) and "John Berryman's Bridge" (first appeared in _The Unrealist_). The latter poem is included in _Periods of Lucidity_, © 1978 by Joseph Barrett.

Coleman Barks for "A Section of The Oconee Near Watkinsville" and "Broomstraw."

Carley Rees Bogarad for "My Father's Black Lungs" (first appeared in _A Magazine Of Appalachian Women_).

Joe Basilone for "12/31/59-1/1/70."

Susan Burgess for "An Interpretation."

Marita Garin for "Dogwood Tree" (first appeared in *Intro 10*, © The Associated Writing Programs) and "Climbing to Linville Falls" (first appeared in *The Arts Journal*, July 1980).

Sharon Ginsburg for "Final Strength."

James B. Goode for "Poets of Darkness" from *Poets of Darkness*. University Press of Mississippi, © 1981 by James B. Goode.

Pat Gray for "Couple."

Richard Hague for "Snag" and "Lesson" from *Crossings*, Cincinnati Area Poetry Press, © 1978 by Richard Hague.

Pauletta Hansel for "January Sky Like Bedsheets."

Harper and Row for "The Beans" and "For the Anniversary of My Father's Death" from *Years That Answer*, © 1980 by Margaret A. Anderson.

Marc Harshman for "First Cutting" from *Turning Out the Stones*, State Street Press, © 1983 by Marc Harshman.

Vicky Hayes for "Wire Wizard."

Sherry Holstein for "A Woman Too Big for Her House" (first appeared in *A Magazine of Appalachian Women*).

Mike Henson for "Wonder Women."

Ira Herman for "Small Tragedies in Civilized Places..." and "Rendezvous" from *Dark Horses Leaping into Flame*, © 1978 by Northwoods Press.

Lee Howard for "The Last Unmined Vein" from *The Last Unmined Vein*, © 1980 by Lee Howard and Anemone Press.

Dolores Jacobs for "Living in Appalachia" (first appeared in *Tennessee Voices*, 1980-81 Yearbook).

David Jarvis for "Spring Fever" and "Snapshots."

Carey Jobe for "The Kelly's Reunion."

Loyal Jones for "From Melvin Isaacs" (first appeared in *Appalachian Heritage*).

Rodney Jones for "American Forest" and "Dulcimer" from *The Story They Told Us of Light*, University of Alabama Press, © 1980.

Jane Wilson Joyce for "Life and Art in East Tennessee" (first appeared in *Adena*, Fall 1980).

Sheila Joyce for "Rivers."

Louisana State University Press for "My Grandmother Washes Her Vessels" by Fred Chappell, from *Midquest*, LSU, 1982.

George Ella Lyon for "Her Words" and "How the Letters Bloom..." from *Mountain*, Andrew Mountain Press, Hartford, CT, © 1983.

Russell Marano for "Flora" from *Poems from a Mountain Ghetto*, Back Fork Books, Webster, West Virginia, © 1979.

Adrianne Marcus for "The Beginning."

Jeff Daniel Marion for "In a Southerly Direction" and "Ebbing and Flowing Spring" from *Out in the Country, Back Home,* Jackpine Press, Winston-Salem, NC, 1976.

Margaret McDowell for "Jelly Bread."

Michael McFee for "Reclamation" and "Signs and Wonders."

Bonni McKeown for "Legacy's Daughter" from *Pieces*, Mountain State Press, Charleston, West Virginia, c. 1982 (first appeared in *The Unrealist*, No. 3, 1981).

Llewellyn McKernan for "Mother Milking" from *Short and Simple Annals*, © 1979.

Devon McNamara for "Fossil Fuel."

Louise McNeill for "The New Corbies" from *Paradox Hill: From Appalachia to Lunar Shore*, West Virginia University Foundation, 1972.

Alice McNew for "Old Bodine Crow."

Evelyn Miller for "On Meeting Ferlinghetti's Mortician."

Heather Ross Miller for "The Vinegar Jug" and "Lumbee Children" from *Horse Horse, Tyger Tyger,* Red Clay Books, 1974.

Jim Wayne Miller for "The Brier Losing Touch with His Traditions" and "Living with Children" from The Mountains Have Come Closer, Appalachian Consortium Press, 1980.

Elizabeth Moore for "An Old Story—Retold."

Janice Townley Moore for "The Way Back."

Maureen Morehead for "Chad" (first appeared in *Twigs*, Fall 1976).

Allan Morgan for "And All Those Naked Men."

Robert Morgan and Gnomon Press for "Canning Time" from *Groundwork*, Gnomon, 1979.

Donald Narkevic for "The Engagement."

W.W. Norton for "Chestnut," by Robert Morgan from *Red Owl*, Norton, 1972.

Lee Pennington for "Train Horn" from *Scenes from a Southern Road*, JRD Publishing Company, 1969.

Rita Quillen for "Discovered," (first appeared in *The Mockingbird*, vol. VI, 1979).

Larry Richman for "The Joys of House Wrecking."

Anne Roney for "Spring Leaffall" (first appeared in *The Small Farm*) and "Gift Card."

John Russell for "Afternoon at the Sportsman," from *Strokes: Contemporary Appalachian Poetry*, Chain SAWC Press, Richmond, WV, 1980.

Timothy Russell for "The Porch and the Sycamore."

Bettie M. Sellers for "Bluegrass Interval" and "Mycenae" from *Morning of the Red-Tailed Hawk*, Green River Press, 1981.

Susan Sheppard for "Song from the Distant Native," (first appeared in *Backcountry*, 1978.

Betsy Sholl for "Convalescence" from *Appalachian Winter*, Alice James Books, 1978, and for "The Flood" (first appeared in *West Branch*).

Larry Simpson for "Clearing the Way" (first appeared in *Mountain Review*).

Bennie Lee Sinclair for "Landmark" and "My Grandmother" from *The Arrowhead Scholar*, © 1978.

Barbara Smith for "Lines" and "Century #1, Portrait of a Coaltown."

Dave Smith for "The Luminosity for Life" from *Cumberland Station*, University of Illinois Press, © 1976.

Bob Snyder for "Poem for Aunt Rebecca" and "No Regrets" from *We'll See Who's a Peasant*, Mountain Union Books, Beckley, West Virginia, 1977.

Charlotte St. John for "The Square Dance."

Paul Curry Steele for "Mrs. Henritze" from *Anse on Island Creek*, Mountain State Press, Charleston, West Virginia, 1981.

Jim Stokely for "Coal" and "This Land, Full of Said Regions" from *Mummy Truths*, Southbound Books, Knoxville, Tennessee, 1978.

195

Charles Wright for "Sentences" and "January," both from *China Trace*, Wesleyan University Press, 1977.

Barbara Yount for "Requiem" from *No Business Poems*, Reynolds Homestead, Critz, West Virginia.

Isabel Zuber for "In a Quiet Larder" and "From the Garlic Patch" from *No Business Poems*, Reynolds Homestead, Critz, West Virginia.

The Editors

Bob Henry Baber

George Ella Lyon

Gurney Norman

THE JESSE STUART FOUNDATION

Incorporated in 1979 for public, charitable, and educational purposes, the Jesse Stuart Foundation is devoted to preserving both Jesse Stuart's literary legacy and W-Hollow, the eastern Kentucky valley which became a part of America's literary landscape as a result of Stuart's writings. The Foundation, which controls rights to Stuart's published and unpublished literary works, is currently reprinting many of his best out-of-print books, along with other books which focus on Kentucky and Southern Appalachia.

Our primary purpose is to publish books which supplement the educational system, at all levels. We have now produced more than thirty editions and have hundreds of other regional books in stock, because we want to make these materials accessible to students, teachers, librarians, and general readers. We also promote Stuart's legacy through video tapes, dramas, and presentations for school and civic groups.

Stuart taught and lectured extensively. His teaching experience ranged from the one-room schoolhouses of his youth in eastern Kentucky to the American University in Cairo, Egypt, and embraced years of service as school superintendent, high-school teacher, and high-school principal. "First, last, always," said Jesse Stuart, "I am a teacher ... Good teaching is forever and the teacher is immortal."

In keeping with Stuart's devotion to teaching, the Jesse Stuart Foundation is working hard to publish materials that will be appropriate for school use. For example, the Foundation has reprinted seven of Stuart's junior books (for grades 3-6), and a Teacher's Guide to assist with their classroom use. The Foundation has also published several books that would be appropriate for grades 6-12: Stuart's *Hie to the Hunters*, Thomas D. Clark's *Simon Kenton, Kentucky Scout*, and Billy C. Clark's *A Long Row To Hoe*. Other recent JSF publications range from college history texts to books for adult literacy students.

James M. Gifford
Executive Director